I0449181

Use design
to design
change

Use Design to Design Change

Second Edition

Copyright © 2024 James Hurst

All rights reserved.

No part of this book may be reproduced, stored in a retrieval system, or transmitted in any form or by any means—electronic, mechanical, photocopying, recording, or otherwise—without prior written permission from the author, except for the inclusion of brief quotations in a review.

Published by Rogue School

ISBN: 978-1-300-77247-7

Printed in USA

First Edition: 2022 & Second Edition: 2024

For permissions, inquiries, or more information, please visit www.rogue.school

# Hello

I'm James, a creative director and brand strategist with a career spanning over two decades. I've influenced the design and branding of many organizations—some you'll love (and some you won't). Along the way, I've helped shape visual identities and brand narratives as Head of Brand Design at Google, Global Creative Director at Pinterest, Creative Director at Tinder, Principal at DesignStudio, and more.

I'm profoundly committed to education and thought leadership. I've developed and taught courses on using artificial intelligence to enhance aesthetic intelligence. I've nurtured nascent ideas from inception to fruition and advised established brands on scaling and adaptation.

I define a brand as a comprehensive business operating system and find it triggering when people say "brand" but mean "visual identity." I use the triple bottom line to ensure intentionality in brand-building—creating brands that benefit people, planet, and profit—while encouraging a holistic approach that considers historical context, natural systems, and contemporary dynamics.

My wife, Sophie, and my kids—Millie, Iris, and Freddie—are my everything and my greatest inspiration. Thank you for being such incredible teachers, playmates, soulmates, and friends.

I owe immense gratitude to the many colleagues and communities I've been lucky to play alongside. To the First Things Club and Bonfire With Soul—thank you. A special thanks to Duke Stump for being such a guiding light, and to Maria Raga and Matt Leta for providing critical feedback when I needed it most. Anything smart in this book is thanks to you. Shortcomings and mistakes are all on me.

Writing this second edition has been an absolute pleasure. I really hope you get a kick out of it. XX

# Contents

# Designing Change

On a quiet morning in April 1970, Gary Anderson sat at his drafting table, sketching ideas for a design competition. The brief was simple: create a symbol to promote recycling. Anderson's vision took shape as three arrows chasing one another in a continuous loop, symbolizing the endless cycle of reuse. He couldn't have imagined that his design would transcend its initial purpose, becoming a universal symbol for sustainability and a powerful catalyst for change. It was a symbol that distilled a complex concept into a clear and compelling visual—a reminder of how simple ideas, executed well, can change the world.

It's why I became a brand designer.

In a time when products are replicated overnight and technologies rapidly become obsolete, what sets enduring brands apart isn't just their ability to innovate; it's their ability to infuse meaning into everything they do. Research and development budgets may produce groundbreaking features, but those features can be copied. Prices can be undercut, markets can shift, and technologies will always evolve. Amid all this turbulence, the one thing that remains is the brand—the essence that defines it, the emotions it evokes, the relationships it fosters, and the changes it inspires. A brand that knows its purpose doesn't simply sell products; it shapes culture, influences behavior, and leaves a lasting imprint on society.

In 2006, Blake Mycoskie visited Argentina and saw children walking barefoot on dusty streets. Instead of simply sympathizing, he took action. He founded TOMS with a one-for-one model: for every pair of shoes purchased, a pair would be donated to a child in need. It wasn't just about making shoes; it was about fostering compassion and mobilizing customers to become part of a broader mission. Suddenly, buying a pair of shoes was not just a transaction—it was an act of empathy, a small but impactful step toward change. The brand became a movement, fueled by a purpose that resonated deeply with people who wanted to make a difference.

Some brands have a profound resonance because they tap into something essential: the desire for individuals to be part of something bigger than themselves. This is what drives them to form communities rather than just customer bases. The most successful brands transcend the transaction; they become symbols of shared values and common aspirations.

The world today is changing at an unprecedented pace, with movements like Extinction Rebellion and Occupy Wall Street sparking massive shifts in societal conversations. These weren't polished campaigns crafted in boardrooms; they were raw and authentic expressions of collective frustration, driven by conviction rather than strategic planning. Extinction Rebellion began with an urgent, unscripted plea on the streets of London, and Occupy Wall Street started with a simple call to gather in a park. Their imperfect beginnings remind us that change rarely starts with flawless execution; it begins with purpose, passion, and a willingness to take the first step, no matter how uncertain.

This principle finds powerful echoes in the business world. Amazon launched in a garage with a bold vision to sell books online—a revolutionary idea at a time when the internet was still a curiosity. Google introduced its search engine as a minimalist page in a cluttered digital environment, focusing on simplicity and utility. These companies didn't wait until their offerings were perfect; they moved forward with conviction, trusting in their ability to adapt and improve over time.

Purpose, as it turns out, isn't a final destination; it's a journey that demands constant adaptation. Netflix's evolution from a DVD rental service to a streaming giant—and later, a content producer—exemplifies the power of embracing change. The company wasn't afraid to disrupt itself, to pivot, and to take risks when the moment demanded it. Netflix remained guided by a core culture that valued risk, innovation, and a willingness to change in the face of an evolving industry.

This book is for those who want to build brands that go beyond profit margins—brands that matter, that design change rather than simply responding to it. The power of design extends far beyond making something visually appealing; it is a force for solving problems, connecting people, and creating lasting value. Through design, brands can engage with real challenges, build meaningful connections, and establish a legacy that endures.

Throughout these pages, we will explore how to launch with courage, scale with deliberate intention, and adapt with resilience. We will dive into stories from the edges of society—stories that reveal how unconventional thinking leads to extraordinary outcomes. From protest movements that reframe societal norms to biomimicry principles that redefine what is possible in design, these examples offer inspiration and practical lessons.

This journey is not for those seeking the comfort of conformity. Building a brand with purpose requires a willingness to question entrenched beliefs, to embrace ambiguity, and often to take the road less traveled. It requires making deliberate choices that defy convention but are rooted in the brand's core values. There are no shortcuts; only a path shaped by clear purpose and the courage to act.

This book is for entrepreneurs ready to challenge the status quo, creatives eager to explore uncharted territory, leaders determined to inspire teams, and anyone who believes that business can be a force for good. It's for those who have grown weary of playing it safe, who are ready to build something that matters—something resilient, something impactful.

Let's begin by embracing a simple, profound idea: design is not merely about creating things; it is about making things happen. It is about envisioning a better future and taking deliberate steps toward bringing that future to life. The time to act is now, with courage, conviction, and creativity. The change we want to see begins with the choices we make and the designs we create.

Together, we can forge a path forward, one that challenges the status quo, inspires action, and makes an enduring impact. The question is not whether change will happen; it is whether we will take the lead in shaping it.

# Chapter 1:
# **Launch**

In the summer of 2007, two young designers in San Francisco were trying to figure out how to make rent. A major design conference was coming to town, and the hotels were fully booked. They saw an opportunity: why not rent out air mattresses in their living room to attendees who needed a place to stay? They called it "AirBed & Breakfast."

Brian Chesky and Joe Gebbia had no way of knowing that this modest experiment would spark a revolution in hospitality. Airbnb didn't start with venture capital funding or a detailed business plan. It started with a need, a creative solution, and the courage to see what might happen if they just began.

The act of launching—of taking that first step—is powerful because it defies the comfort of planning, the safety of certainty. So often, we think of beginnings as carefully orchestrated events, backed by solid guarantees. Yet, the truth is that the world-changing ideas often emerge not because everything is perfectly aligned, but because someone simply decided to start.

In August 2018, a fifteen-year-old girl named Greta Thunberg decided she wouldn't go to school. Instead, she stood alone outside the Swedish parliament with a sign that read "School Strike for Climate." Greta wasn't looking to lead a global movement; she was frustrated, and this was her way of expressing it. But her solitary act caught attention, and Fridays for Future was born, mobilizing millions of young people to demand climate action.

There is something undeniably compelling about those moments when someone decides to launch— to act—without knowing where the road might lead. It's a leap of faith that seems to defy common sense but carries the potential to change everything.

Take Google Maps. When it was introduced in 2005, it wasn't the comprehensive tool we all rely on today. It was basic, a work in progress. But by releasing it to the public, Google invited users into the process of its evolution. Every interaction provided data, feedback, and insights that helped refine the product over time. It wasn't polished, but it was out there—and that made all the difference.

Or think of the Zapatista movement in Mexico. On January 1, 1994, a group of indigenous activists declared war against the Mexican government, protesting the implementation of NAFTA and the marginalization of their communities. They had limited resources and no major international backing, but they used the nascent internet to amplify their message. It worked. Their voices reached a global audience and drew attention to issues that had been ignored for far too long.

These examples share a common thread: they show that the power of launching lies in the act itself—in beginning before you're ready. You don't need all the answers. You just need to start.

The biggest barrier to launching is often fear. Fear of failure, of ridicule, of the unknown. It's easy to wait for perfect conditions, but perfect rarely comes. The founders of Airbnb could have dismissed their idea as too simplistic. Greta could have stayed in school, hoping someone else would take action. The Zapatistas could have remained silent, accepting their circumstances.

But they didn't. They acted. And their actions rippled outward, creating impacts they couldn't have anticipated.

Momentum builds when action meets purpose. Airbnb has grown into a global platform connecting millions of travelers with hosts around the world. Greta Thunberg has become a leading voice for climate action. The

Zapatista movement inspired countless activists and brought international awareness to indigenous rights.

So, what stops us from taking that first step? Often, it's the pursuit of perfection or the comfort of endless planning. But meaningful change starts not with certainty but with courage. Launching something is not about having everything figured out; it's about embracing the unknown, recognizing that the perfect moment may never come, and starting anyway.

For every success story, there are countless ideas that never take flight. The difference isn't always the quality of the idea—it's the willingness to begin. Some social movements fade before they even take root because the fear of imperfection outweighs the desire to make a difference. The potential impact gets buried under layers of hesitation.

But there are ways to set yourself up for success, to make that first leap less daunting. One of the simplest steps is to share your idea—to invite others into the process. Launching doesn't have to mean going public on a massive scale; it can be as small as asking for feedback, testing a concept, or putting a prototype into the world.

Today, there are countless tools and platforms that make it easier to gauge whether an idea has traction. You can set up a fake front door—a simple landing page—to see if people are interested in what you're offering. You can run mini ad campaigns for as little as a few dollars a day to understand what resonates. You can spend $100 to validate an idea before committing $1,000, and you can use that $1,000 to build conviction before investing $10,000 more.

Building a roadmap with clear milestones helps ensure that each step you take is purposeful, that you're building confidence along the way. It's about making sure there's a "there" there, but also about keeping the momentum alive—taking action, learning, and adjusting.

In this era, we also have AI tools that can help stress-test our thinking. You can create personas to simulate how different audiences might react to your idea. You can run a quick De

Bono Six Thinking Hats exercise to see your idea from multiple perspectives. You can dive into the semiotics of the visual language you're considering, getting immediate insights into what might resonate. These tools are powerful not because they provide definitive answers, but because they help you iterate, refine, and launch with a stronger foundation.

Launching with conviction doesn't require perfection. It requires intention, adaptability, and the courage to start. It requires believing that what you're doing matters enough to take that first step, even if you don't have all the answers. So, if there's an idea you've been sitting on, a change you want to see—start now. Launch it. Test it. Invite others into the journey.

Ready? Let's go.

# Chapter 2:
# The Power
# of "And"

When faced with decisions, we often see our options as binary: Do we choose quality or speed? Innovation or reliability? As if standing at a crossroads, we feel forced to pick one path and abandon the other. But what if these aren't real choices at all?

In the early 2000s, a small company called Tesla found itself confronting an industry dominated by gas-guzzling giants. The consensus was that a car couldn't be both high-performance and environmentally friendly. Elon Musk and his team refused to accept this dichotomy. Why couldn't an electric vehicle be powerful, stylish, and sustainable?

The Tesla Roadster was the answer to this question. It was a sleek sports car that could accelerate from zero to sixty in under four seconds, without a drop of gasoline. By embracing the power of "and," Tesla redefined what an electric car could be. They showed that performance and sustainability weren't mutually exclusive—they could elevate one another.

This rejection of false choices isn't new. In the mid-1970s, Steve Wozniak dreamed of building a personal computer. At the time, computers were bulky, expensive machines designed for universities and corporations. They were powerful but inaccessible. When Wozniak teamed up with Steve Jobs, they envisioned something different: a computer that was both advanced and easy to use. The Apple I, and later the Apple II, embodied this vision. They didn't settle for either sophistication or simplicity; they found a way to offer both. It was this union that would lead to a revolution in personal technology.

We tend to fall into the trap of "either-or" thinking because it simplifies complex problems. It makes decision-making feel more manageable and less uncertain. But the truth is, it also blinds us to possibilities that exist when we challenge those artificial boundaries.

Consider the concept of social entrepreneurship. Traditional wisdom held that businesses existed to make a profit, while nonprofits were there to serve social causes. Muhammad Yunus, an economist from Bangladesh, saw the potential to merge these two worlds. In 1983, he founded Grameen Bank, providing microloans to impoverished entrepreneurs without requiring collateral. Yunus didn't see profitability and social impact as mutually exclusive; instead, he fused them into a sustainable model that lifted millions out of poverty. Grameen Bank was not just a financial institution—it was a testament to the power of "and."

Embracing "and" can unlock innovative solutions. In 1969, when NASA set out to put a man on the moon, they couldn't choose between speed and safety—both were essential. The Apollo program demanded technological breakthroughs that defied existing limitations. Refusing to accept trade-offs led to one of humanity's greatest achievements.

In 2010, the eyewear industry was dominated by a few large players, and consumers paid the price. The founders of Warby Parker imagined something different: a brand that offered both affordability and style. By designing glasses in-house and selling directly to customers online, they cut costs without compromising quality. They also introduced a "Buy a Pair, Give a Pair" program, donating glasses to those in need for every pair sold. Profitability and social responsibility became intertwined.

Saying "yes, and" is a skill taught in improv theater. It's about building on ideas rather than shutting them down. This principle is powerful in business, too. At the early stages of an idea, it's crucial to remain open—to explore every avenue rather than prematurely narrowing your focus. Once a company or movement has taken hold, it can afford to specialize and refine, but at the beginning, embracing the power of "and" can mean the difference between success and stagnation.

History is full of examples of movements that failed because they couldn't break free of "either-or" thinking. Opportunities slipped away because of premature gatekeeping or an unwillingness to adapt. In contrast, successful ideas tend to grow when they're given room to breathe, when they evolve organically, embracing all the possibilities available.

To cultivate this mindset in your own endeavors, start by reframing the questions you ask. When faced with two appealing but seemingly incompatible options, ask how you might achieve both. This doesn't mean ignoring real-world constraints, but it does encourage creative problem-solving that moves beyond limiting assumptions.

There are tools and frameworks to help people unlock the power of "and" in the early phases of an idea. Design thinking, for example, emphasizes empathy, ideation, and prototyping—all geared toward breaking down binary thinking and finding solutions that merge competing needs. The "Both/And" technique, used in negotiation and leadership, helps people hold multiple truths at once, encouraging richer and more nuanced solutions. These approaches are validated, not because they ignore constraints, but because they help reimagine them.

And now, we have AI. Tools like ChatGPT can help you explore the "and" when your mind feels stuck in "either-or." You can use AI to draft ideas that combine seemingly opposing forces, stress-test concepts with different personas, or even visualize how an idea might evolve in various scenarios. AI can help ensure that you and your team aren't prematurely shutting down opportunities. It can enable a growth culture—one that's open, iterative, and constantly climbing toward something new—rather than a defensive one that clings to what it already has.

The power of "and" is about seeing beyond the artificial barriers that hold us back. It's about imagining a world where we don't have to choose between good and better—where we can have both, and in doing so, create something extraordinary. By embracing this mindset, we unlock not just innovative products and brands but also new ways of thinking that can transform industries and communities.

If you find yourself standing at a crossroads, feeling forced to choose, take a moment to reconsider. What might happen if you said "yes" to both? The answer could be the key to something remarkable.

# Chapter 3:
# The Cultist Conundrum

In the 1970s, a small computer company in Cupertino, California began to attract a kind of devotion that was unheard of for a tech firm. Apple wasn't merely selling machines; it was creating an identity. Customers didn't just use Apple products—they evangelized them. They wore Apple t-shirts, adorned their cars with Apple stickers, and lined up overnight for the latest release.

What makes a brand inspire loyalty so fervent that it borders on fanaticism? How does it cultivate that kind of devotion, and, more importantly, how does it avoid the risks inherent in such loyalty?

Enter CrossFit. Founded in 2000 by Greg Glassman, it began as a single gym in Santa Cruz, offering an unorthodox, high-intensity regimen. In just a few years, CrossFit expanded into a global phenomenon, boasting over 13,000 affiliate gyms by 2020. CrossFit didn't advertise in the conventional sense; it built a community. Members adopted a distinct lexicon—terms like AMRAPs, WODs, and EMOMs—and cultivated a shared identity. They weren't just exercising; they were part of a movement.

But with intense loyalty comes risk. In 2020, remarks made by Glassman led to widespread outrage and disaffiliation by many gyms and athletes. CrossFit's identity was so closely tied to its founder that his actions threatened the entire community. This incident highlighted a critical question for brands that cultivate passionate communities: How do you build a sense of belonging that is empowering, without letting it slide into cult-like exclusivity?

The line between community and cult can be thin. Brands that build strong communities do so by tapping into fundamental human needs: belonging, identity, and purpose. They create spaces where people feel valued and part of something greater than themselves. Patagonia, for instance, doesn't just sell outdoor gear—it advocates for environmental causes. Customers wear Patagonia not just for the quality, but for what it represents: a commitment to preserving the planet.

Yet, the same strategies that foster deep connection can lead to insularity. When a brand becomes central to someone's identity, criticism feels personal, and dissenting voices become threats. This echo chamber stifles growth and leaves the community vulnerable to blind spots.

Harley-Davidson, for example, faced bankruptcy in the early 1980s. Their response was to focus not just on selling motorcycles but on cultivating a lifestyle. The Harley Owners Group (HOG) was established, rallying riders around a shared passion. Harley-Davidson merchandise and organized events transformed customers into lifelong advocates. Crucially, though, Harley understood the need for inclusivity. They didn't gatekeep who could be a part of the community. New riders were welcomed, and the brand evolved to include a diverse range of customers. By balancing tradition with openness, they maintained loyalty without creating a closed-off cult.

Contrast this with Theranos, the infamous biotech startup founded by Elizabeth Holmes. Promising to revolutionize blood testing, Theranos operated in extreme secrecy. The culture discouraged questioning and silenced dissent. Holmes cultivated an aura of infallibility, which prevented critical voices from surfacing. The outcome was disastrous—when the technology failed, the company crumbled. The lack of transparency and intolerance for criticism led directly to its downfall.

The difference lies in transparency and humility. Brands that encourage questioning, invite feedback, and admit mistakes build genuine trust. Loyalty isn't about blind devotion; it's about mutual respect. REI's decision to close its stores on Black Friday and encourage people to spend the day outdoors wasn't just a marketing ploy. It was a reflection of their values— an invitation for their community to join them in something bigger than commerce. It resonated because it was authentic.

The challenge—the Cultist Conundrum—is navigating the fine line between fostering passionate loyalty and slipping into the pitfalls of exclusion and dogma. The passion that drives someone to launch an idea can easily become an obsession. People can fall into a cult of their own idea, convinced of its rightness to the exclusion of all else.

This is where the distinction between extrinsic and intrinsic thinking becomes vital. Extrinsic benefits are tangible, often transactional: "This product will save you time." Intrinsic benefits, on the other hand, tap into deeper motivations: "This product will give you more time to spend with the people you love." Moving from extrinsic to intrinsic requires getting to the heart of why an idea matters—why it resonates at a human level.

Often, this shift is expressed as moving from features to benefits. Features are what a product does; benefits are why it matters to the user. Apple understood this when they marketed the iPod not as a device with "5GB of storage" but as "1,000 songs in your pocket." The feature was the storage capacity; the benefit was the experience it offered.

The conviction that founders feel is crucial for bringing an idea into the world. It's what gives an idea momentum. But that conviction must be balanced with openness—a willingness to understand how others see value in what you're offering. Cults play on intrinsic ideals, creating an emotional connection so strong that members can overlook inconsistencies or flaws. In branding, tapping into intrinsic motivations can help identify the core human truth that makes your product meaningful. But unlike a cult, you must remain open to critique, ready to adapt, and aware of the limits of your perspective.

To help move from extrinsic features to intrinsic benefits, there are frameworks designed to clarify this transformation. The "Jobs to Be Done" framework is one such tool—it encourages you to think about what job your product is being hired to do in someone's life. It shifts the focus from what the product is to what the product enables. Similarly, Simon Sinek's concept of "Start With Why" helps founders articulate the deeper purpose behind their work—not just what they do, but why it matters.

Today, we can also use AI to help push this kind of thinking further. AI can serve as a sparring partner, challenging you to articulate why your idea matters, who it matters to, and how best to express that value. By running through scenarios, creating personas, or testing different messaging strategies, AI can help stress-test your thinking and ensure you're not falling into the trap of insularity. It can help you expand beyond the feature set, pushing toward a narrative that captures the true benefit—one that resonates on a deeply human level.

Brands that cultivate loyalty without falling into the Cultist Conundrum embrace transparency, openness, and the power of intrinsic connection. They inspire not because they demand unwavering devotion, but because they invite people into a shared journey—a journey defined by growth, honesty, and a vision that evolves.

The goal isn't to create followers who never question. It's to inspire believers who are so aligned with your mission that they're willing to help you grow, adapt, and thrive. That's how you build something that lasts—not a cult, but a community.

# Chapter 4
# **Writing Your Legacy**

In 1971, Jim Collins joined Hewlett-Packard fresh from Stanford, eager to make his mark. During his early days at the company, he found himself exploring its archives, where he stumbled on a letter written by David Packard, one of HP's co-founders. In that letter, Packard articulated a philosophy that would deeply resonate with Collins: "A company has a greater responsibility than making money; it has a responsibility to its employees, its customers, and the community." This simple yet profound idea—that a business can and should be a force for good—set Collins on a lifelong journey. It became the cornerstone of his books like Built to Last and Good to Great, in which he explored how companies endure over time and leave lasting imprints on the world around them.

Building a legacy goes beyond size or profitability. It's about the impact you make, the values you instill, and the enduring mark you leave on people, communities, and society. A legacy is something crafted through every decision, action, and value-driven commitment made over the course of a lifetime. In 2022, Yvon Chouinard showed us what it looks like to build a lasting legacy when he transferred ownership of Patagonia to a trust and nonprofit dedicated to combating the climate crisis. Declaring, "Earth is now our only shareholder," Chouinard ensured that Patagonia's mission to protect the planet would outlive him. This wasn't a spur-of-the-moment decision; it was the culmination of decades of aligning Patagonia's business practices with environmental values, from sourcing sustainable materials to encouraging customers to buy less. Through this singular act, Chouinard secured his legacy—a legacy built on stewardship, activism, and long-term responsibility.

Legacy, however, is not reserved for founders or CEOs. It can be built by anyone with a vision and the courage to act. In 1977, Wangari Maathai, a Kenyan environmentalist, saw how deforestation was ravaging her community. She launched the Green Belt Movement as a response to the environmental degradation and the hardships it caused. What started as a small initiative to plant trees and restore the environment soon grew into a powerful movement that ultimately planted over 51 million trees. Maathai's legacy was not just in the forests she helped to restore; it was in the lives she transformed and the model she created for empowering communities. In 2004, her pioneering work was recognized with the Nobel Peace Prize, honoring her contribution to both environmental and human development.

The stories of Yvon Chouinard and Wangari Maathai remind us of a common theme—a commitment to something greater than personal success or profit. Writing a legacy often requires making choices that defy conventional business logic, prioritizing long-term impact over short-term gains. Sometimes, it demands personal sacrifice. In 1967, at the height of his career, Muhammad Ali refused to be drafted into the U.S. military during the Vietnam War. He cited religious and ethical objections, and the repercussions were immense. Ali was stripped of his heavyweight title, faced possible imprisonment, and was banned from boxing for three years. But his stance defined him as more than an athlete; it defined him as a champion of civil rights, a symbol of courage, and an icon of integrity. "I know where I'm going and I know the truth," Ali said. "I don't have to be what you want me to be." In choosing to live by his values, regardless of the cost, he secured a legacy of conviction and purpose.

For those inspired to craft their own legacy, the journey starts with clarifying values. What do you stand for? What principles are non-negotiable? This step goes far beyond writing a catchy mission statement; it requires a deep reflection on the beliefs that form the foundation of who you are and how you operate. Values are the compass that guides every decision, large or small. Defining them means being deliberate about what matters most to you and your brand—whether it's sustainability, creativity, equality, or something else entirely.

Once values are clearly defined, the next step is alignment. Actions must consistently align with those core principles. Consistency breeds trust, and trust, in turn, amplifies impact. Ben & Jerry's, for example, doesn't speak out on social issues as a marketing strategy; it's a natural extension of the values the company has upheld for decades. By integrating social responsibility into their business model, they have built an authentic connection with consumers who value integrity and action. Their legacy, therefore, isn't just about ice cream; it's about activism, justice, and a commitment to change.

Beyond clarifying values and aligning actions, creating a legacy demands a long-term perspective. Legacies are not constructed overnight; they are cultivated through years of sustained effort, a willingness to adapt, and an understanding of the larger picture. In the world of technology, where companies often rise and fall rapidly, the ones that leave a lasting impact are those that see beyond quarterly returns. Steve Jobs built Apple into a technology giant by focusing on products that were not only functional but also beautiful and intuitive. Jobs was not without his critics—his leadership style was often labeled as abrasive, and he faced numerous setbacks along the way—but his enduring impact on technology, design, and the way we interact with the world defined his legacy. A legacy is not about perfection; it's about the impact you create and the ways in which you change the world.

Resilience and the ability to adapt in the face of setbacks are key components of a lasting legacy. Nelson Mandela spent 27 years in prison, and yet emerged to lead South Africa as its first Black president. His legacy is a story of resilience, forgiveness, and unwavering dedication to justice and reconciliation. It wasn't about how quickly he achieved his goals; it was about his ability to persevere and stay true to his vision over decades. In a world focused on immediate gains and rapid growth, it is these long-term visions that stand the test of time.

To build a meaningful legacy, it's helpful to ask questions that reach deep into your core motivations and your long-term vision. What kind of difference do you want to make in the world? How do your actions today contribute to that larger goal? What will people say about your impact when you're no longer in the room? Answering these questions helps to frame a legacy not as an abstract concept, but as a series of tangible actions that accumulate over time.

One framework for defining a personal or brand legacy is the "Legacy Ladder," which moves from individual principles to broader societal impact. Start by defining your core values—those beliefs that you would not compromise, even under pressure. Then, think about how these values can manifest in actions within your organization or community. Finally, extend those actions to envision the kind of broader impact you wish to have. By climbing this ladder, you can begin to see how small, value-driven decisions accumulate into something that lasts beyond your own time.

Another tool is to use AI to help envision speculative futures. By utilizing AI-driven scenario planning, individuals and organizations can create multiple potential futures that help visualize what a legacy might look like. Tools like narrative AI generators can be used to write speculative stories about the impact of your brand or your personal work—imagining, for instance, a newspaper article written ten years in the future that celebrates the changes you've helped create. This type of exercise allows you to articulate a desired future state and then work backward, setting milestones to ensure that your current actions are leading you toward that vision.

AI can also be used to analyze patterns and identify potential pitfalls in pursuing a particular legacy path. By examining historical data, market trends, and cultural shifts, AI can provide insights into what kind of impact is likely to be lasting and where the risks of being misunderstood or facing backlash might lie. This insight can help refine the path to building a meaningful legacy, ensuring it remains aligned with your core values while also being responsive to changes in the world.

Thinking of the long-term impact and working back from

a desired future is a powerful exercise in intentionality. When you can imagine how people will talk about the work you've done—whether it's a community project, a brand, or an entire movement—you can then create a set of milestones to make that imagined future a reality. It allows you to make deliberate, short-term plans that align with the big-picture vision, ensuring that each step taken today is contributing to an enduring impact.

Writing a legacy, then, is about more than just looking back with pride. It's about shaping what is yet to come. It's about clarifying your values, aligning your actions, and making decisions that prioritize significance over immediate gains. It's about recognizing that legacy is not just what you leave behind for others—it's what you leave within people, the inspiration, courage, and values that endure in their lives. Through this deliberate approach, the goal becomes not simply to build a brand or achieve success, but to craft something that resonates, something that lasts, something that genuinely matters.

The path to building a legacy is not always easy. It requires resilience, adaptability, and a willingness to take risks. But the rewards—the opportunity to make an enduring positive impact—are worth every sacrifice. By aligning each action with the deepest values, and by taking deliberate, courageous steps toward a bigger vision, we can build legacies worth remembering. Whether through the trees you plant, the products you create, the movements you start, or the inspiration you give, your legacy will be written in the lasting imprint you leave on the world.

# Chapter 5
# **Scale**

In 2004, a small social networking site called Facebook was operating out of a Harvard dorm room. It was a digital yearbook, exclusive to college students, connecting classmates across campus. Mark Zuckerberg and his team faced a pivotal question: How do you take something intimate and personal and expand it without losing its essence?

Scaling isn't just about getting bigger; it's about growing while staying true to your core. It requires clarity of purpose, careful consideration of why you need to scale, and a clear understanding of the benefits and potential pitfalls.

Facebook began by opening its doors to other universities, then to high schools, and eventually to anyone over the age of thirteen. With each expansion, they navigated the delicate balance between growth and user experience. The challenge was clear: Could they maintain the close-knit community feel while serving millions, and eventually billions, of users?

This challenge isn't unique to tech giants. It echoes across industries and organizations of all sizes. Scaling can mean different things depending on your goals—whether it's to make more money, help more people, reduce costs, or become more resilient.

Five Guys, the burger joint that began as a family-owned carry-out shop in Arlington, Virginia. In 1986, Jerry and Janie Murrell focused on one simple mission: make the best burgers and fries possible. For nearly two decades, they operated only a handful of locations, perfecting their product. Then, in 2003, they decided to franchise. Today, Five Guys has over 1,500 locations worldwide. The key to their successful scaling? Simplicity and consistency. No freezers—only coolers. Fresh ingredients delivered daily. A limited menu that allowed them to maintain quality control. Scaling wasn't just about getting bigger; it was about replicating what worked, without losing sight of their core values.

Scaling can also be about impact. Take Doctors Without Borders (Médecins Sans Frontières), founded in 1971 by a small group of French doctors and journalists. The organization aimed to provide medical aid where it was most needed, regardless of political boundaries. As crises erupted around the world, the demand for their services grew. Scaling meant confronting logistical nightmares—coordinating thousands of volunteers, navigating political complexities, and working in dangerous environments. But they stayed anchored to their core principles: neutrality, impartiality, and independence. These values guided them, allowing them to scale their impact without compromising their mission.

Scaling isn't always a success story. WeWork's rapid expansion serves as a cautionary tale. Founded in 2010, WeWork set out to revolutionize office spaces, providing shared work environments with a sense of community. Investors bought into the vision, and the company expanded at breakneck speed, opening locations across the globe. But their focus on growth overshadowed sustainability. WeWork leased expensive properties, invested in extravagant perks, and expanded into businesses that were far removed from their core mission. By 2019, plans for an IPO unraveled amid financial losses and governance issues, and the company's valuation plummeted. Scaling without a solid foundation can lead to collapse.

Nature provides its own lessons on the power and perils of scaling. Think of a forest ecosystem. As trees grow, they create a canopy that allows the entire ecosystem to flourish—more sunlight, more rainwater, and a healthier environment for plants, insects, and animals. But unchecked growth can also lead to imbalance. When a species grows too quickly, it can overtake resources, disrupting the natural harmony.

Scaling requires balance—knowing when to grow, how to expand, and when to hold back. From these examples, there are some important lessons to be learned about scaling effectively.

First, know why you need to scale. Are you scaling to reach more people, to make a bigger impact, to reduce costs, or to improve resilience? Facebook scaled to connect the world; Five Guys scaled to bring quality burgers to a larger audience; Doctors Without Borders scaled to save lives in more places. Knowing your "why" will guide how you approach growth.

Second, learn from the warnings. Scaling too fast, without a solid foundation, can lead to failure. WeWork's downfall came from a lack of focus on sustainable growth. In nature, unchecked growth often ends in collapse— overextended resources and instability. Scaling isn't just about adding more; it's about growing wisely.

To help determine whether or not to scale—and how to do so—there are key frameworks you can use. The "Three Horizons Framework" encourages you to look at growth in three stages: the present (horizon one), the near-term future (horizon two), and the far-off future (horizon three). It helps you ensure that your core remains strong while you explore future opportunities. The "North Star Metric" framework encourages you to identify a single metric that best captures the value you're delivering. By keeping your focus on this key metric, you can guide growth efforts without losing sight of what makes your product or service valuable in the first place.

AI can be an invaluable tool in scaling, not just in automating processes but in stress-testing your strategy. It can help you model different growth scenarios, identify potential bottlenecks, and understand how your core offering might adapt to different market conditions. Imagine using AI to simulate demand under different scaling strategies, helping you anticipate challenges before they become insurmountable.

AI can also be used to plan and test milestones along your scaling journey. Break your scaling strategy into bite-sized steps—an ambitious North Star with realistic, short-term goals. Use AI to track progress, gather feedback, and adjust as needed. Think of AI as a compass, guiding you towards your growth ambitions while keeping you grounded in the reality of what's working and what isn't.

Scaling isn't just about reaching more people; it's about enriching the lives of those you reach. It requires clarity of purpose, adaptability, infrastructure, and culture. It demands an understanding of why growth is necessary and what that growth should achieve. Learn from the successes and failures of others. Reflect on what makes your mission unique. Use tools like AI to ensure you're scaling for the right reasons, with the right strategy.

The path to scaling is full of questions—some inspiring, others daunting. But if you stay true to your purpose, if you grow not just in size but in depth, you'll find that scaling isn't just about numbers. It's about impact. It's about making things better for more people, without losing the soul of what made your endeavor worth scaling in the first place.

# Chapter 6
# The Edge of Relevance

In the mid-1990s, a small startup called Netflix began mailing DVDs to customers. At the time, it was a radical idea that reimagined how people accessed entertainment. They disrupted the traditional video rental industry by eliminating late fees and offering an unparalleled selection of titles. But what set Netflix apart wasn't just the novelty of DVD delivery—it was their ability to evolve ahead of cultural and technological shifts. By the late 2000s, they recognized the potential of streaming media and invested heavily in the infrastructure to make it possible. By 2013, they took yet another leap by producing original content like House of Cards. Critics questioned whether a company built on distribution could succeed in content creation, but Netflix wasn't just reacting to market trends—they were setting them. Today, Netflix stands as one of the world's leading entertainment producers.

This ability to evolve wasn't about guessing what might come next. It was about staying attuned to cultural shifts, technological opportunities, and the essence of what their audience wanted before they even knew to ask for it. What allowed Netflix to thrive while others faded into obscurity was their willingness to challenge conventions, to remain irreverent in the face of assumed wisdom. They refused to be constrained by the categories others placed them in, continuously redefining what they offered and how they connected with audiences. This ability to stay on the edge of relevance—where risk meets opportunity—has become a hallmark of brands that endure.

In 2024, Coca-Cola made a different kind of gamble. Riding the wave of artificial intelligence and the promise of hyper-efficiency in storytelling, they attempted to reimagine their iconic 1995 "Holidays Are Coming" commercial. The original ad, with its glowing red trucks and a jingle that felt like the sonic equivalent of a warm hug, had embedded itself in the collective holiday consciousness. It wasn't just an ad—it was a ritual, a signal that the festive season had officially begun. The new version, created with AI, promised to modernize this tradition, pulling threads from vast datasets to predict what would resonate most. On paper, the strategy was sound. It tested well in focus groups, the AI seamlessly combined elements from years of holiday advertising, and the resulting visuals were crisp, polished, and undeniably modern.

But when the ad hit TikTok, the backlash was immediate and unforgiving. Comments labeled it "creepy holiday vibes" and lamented the absence of the magic that had made the original a cultural cornerstone. The problem wasn't that AI had been used—the world is no stranger to digitally enhanced stories—but that something ineffable was lost in the process. The ad felt like a perfect imitation of joy rather than the real thing. In attempting to optimize tradition, Coca-Cola forgot that sentiment and nostalgia can't be measured in neat, algorithmic terms.

Coca-Cola's stumble reveals a cautionary tale about the limits of AI in creative storytelling. Technology offers tools that can enhance our processes and expand what's possible, but it cannot replace the deeply human intuition required to connect meaningfully with an audience. The "tells" of AI—the moments where something feels too perfect, too polished, too detached from the imperfections of human creativity—can alienate rather than engage. While AI is extraordinary at identifying patterns and simulating emotions, it often fails to grasp the intangible grammar of culture and memory.

This lesson is echoed in the world of gaming, where platforms like Twitch and YouTube Gaming have transformed how people engage with games. Gaming is no longer just about playing; it's about watching, connecting, and storytelling. Twitch's success wasn't driven by perfect graphics or optimized algorithms alone; it emerged from its ability to create authentic spaces where communities could thrive. People didn't just watch gamers—they interacted, shared jokes, and built relationships in real-time chats. The culture wasn't engineered; it was grown, messy and unpredictable in all the ways that make something meaningful.

The edge of relevance is not a space where technology dictates culture, but where culture informs the use of technology. Patagonia offers another powerful example. Yvon Chouinard built the company not just to sell outdoor gear but to inspire environmental stewardship. Every decision—from sourcing materials to launching initiatives like Worn Wear—aligns with this mission. Patagonia's success comes not from chasing trends but from embedding itself within a cultural narrative of responsibility and care. Even as they embrace tools like AI to refine operations and reduce waste, the core remains resolutely human.

The contrast between Netflix's prescient leaps, Patagonia's steadfast intentionality, and Coca-Cola's AI misstep underscores a critical truth: relevance isn't about being new; it's about being meaningful. AI can map trends, test ideas, and simulate outcomes, but it cannot feel. It cannot know the quiet thrill of seeing those red Coca-Cola trucks roll across a snowy landscape or the communal warmth of watching a gamer beat an impossible level while thousands cheer them on. These moments of connection aren't just data points; they are fragments of collective experience.

When brands venture into the terrain of AI, they must ask themselves fundamental questions. Are we using this tool to amplify what we already stand for, or are we using it to replace something that requires a human touch? AI can be a powerful ally in speculative futures, imagining scenarios that stretch the boundaries of what we think is possible. It can refine, iterate, and suggest. But without the grounding of cultural intuition, it risks creating something technically brilliant but emotionally vacant.

The most enduring brands understand that relevance is built through community and co-creation. Supreme, known for its limited-edition drops, doesn't just sell products—it cultivates cultural currency. Its collaborations and intentional scarcity aren't decisions made by algorithms but by people who understand the pulse of their audience. This intentionality is what Coca-Cola missed in its AI-generated ad. In trying to recreate a feeling, they bypassed the human storytellers who might have imbued it with the nuance that algorithms cannot reach.

The edge of relevance is not a comfortable place. It is a place of tension, where the old rubs against the new, and where tradition and innovation must find balance. Brands that thrive here don't chase trends; they set them by deeply understanding what their audience values and then using every tool at their disposal—AI included—to enhance, not replace, that understanding.

Coca-Cola's stumble isn't a death knell for AI in branding, but it is a reminder of the power of restraint. The trucks, the snow, and the jingles that defined the original ad weren't calculated for maximum engagement; they were crafted to evoke something timeless. That is the challenge and the opportunity for brands today: to wield AI not as a crutch but as a collaborator, to extend tradition rather than overwrite it, and to always, always remember the humanity at the heart of relevance.

Netflix, Cirque du Soleil, Twitch, Patagonia—these are not just brands; they are cultural artifacts, deeply embedded in the lives of those who engage with them. The same could have been said for Coca-Cola's trucks. The lesson for any brand venturing to the edge of relevance is clear: the tools may evolve, but the heart of connection is timeless. Use technology wisely, but never let it drown out the soul.

# Chapter 7
# Positioning

In 1975, two college dropouts started a company in a garage in Albuquerque, New Mexico. Paul Allen and Bill Gates had a vision: a computer on every desk in every home. At a time when computers were colossal machines reserved for corporations and universities, their idea seemed absurd. But Microsoft wasn't just another tech company trying to ride the wave of innovation. They were carving out a space that didn't yet exist. By developing software that made computers accessible and user-friendly, they became the bridge between complex technology and everyday users. They didn't just define an industry; they defined a position in the minds of millions.

Positioning isn't just a marketing strategy; it's the art of defining who you are in a way that resonates deeply with your audience. It's about clarity, focus, and the courage to be unapologetically specific. Few brands illustrate this as vividly as Liquid Death, a canned water company founded in 2018 by Mike Cessario.

Cessario, a former punk rocker turned creative director, was struck by how dull and uninspired the bottled water market had become. While energy drinks and beers exuded a rebellious, edgy vibe, water remained trapped in a world of sterile branding and serene blue labels. Cessario saw an opportunity. He envisioned a brand that combined the audacity of a punk rock ethos with an unwavering commitment to sustainability. From this vision, Liquid Death was born—a brand that dared to ask, "What if water wasn't boring?"

Liquid Death's positioning is as bold as its name. With aluminum cans adorned with macabre skulls and heavy metal-inspired typography, the brand is unmistakable. Its mission to "murder your thirst" and "kill plastic pollution" aligns its edgy aesthetic with a meaningful cause: reducing single-use plastic waste. By using recyclable aluminum cans and amplifying its environmental message, Liquid Death carved out a distinct space in the crowded beverage market. Its branding speaks directly to younger consumers disillusioned with sugary drinks and over-processed products, many of whom are also prioritizing environmental responsibility.

This unapologetic stance catapulted Liquid Death from a niche curiosity to a cultural phenomenon. The brand's social media campaigns are equally audacious, featuring absurdist humor, punk rock videos, and collaborations with tattoo artists and musicians. Liquid Death didn't just sell water—it created a movement. Like Microsoft before it, the brand understood that effective positioning isn't about reaching everyone; it's about resonating deeply with the right audience.

Positioning requires authenticity, and that authenticity is born from knowing exactly who you are and who you aren't. Take Swedish oat milk company Oatly, which transformed a humble dairy alternative into a cultural icon. In a market dominated by soy and almond milks, Oatly positioned itself as the champion of a post-milk generation. Their packaging was bold, their messaging irreverent, and their stance on sustainability uncompromising. Like Liquid Death, Oatly embraced a quirky identity that set it apart from competitors.

Brands like Liquid Death and Oatly don't try to please everyone. They speak to those who share their values and humor, forging deep connections with a select group rather than shallow relationships with many. This approach echoes REI's decision to close all stores on Black Friday in 2015, encouraging employees and customers to #OptOutside. By aligning their actions with their values, REI reinforced their position as a brand that prioritizes experiences over consumerism.

Owning your position also means taking risks. Nike demonstrated this in 2018 when it featured Colin Kaepernick in its "Just Do It" campaign. The ad, with its tagline, "Believe in something, even if it means sacrificing everything," polarized audiences. Some customers protested, but Nike's core audience resonated deeply with the message, boosting sales and solidifying the brand's position as a champion of athletes who stand for something bigger than themselves.

However, positioning isn't just about bold campaigns—it's about consistency. IKEA's identity is rooted in democratic design, creating functional and affordable furniture for the masses. Their flat-pack innovation and unpretentious branding reflect this ethos at every touchpoint. In contrast, J.C. Penney faltered in the early 2000s when it abandoned its identity, alienating loyal customers by eliminating sales and coupons. The failed reinvention illustrates the risks of straying from a brand's established position without a clear understanding of its audience.

Liquid Death, in contrast, demonstrates the power of clarity and focus. Its founders didn't just want to sell water; they wanted to create a cultural icon. Every aspect of the brand, from its environmental mission to its punk rock aesthetic, reinforces its identity. This coherence is what transforms brands into movements.

To find and own your position, brands must start by clarifying their core values. Aesop, the Australian skincare brand, built its identity around meticulous attention to detail, from product formulations to minimalist packaging. Similarly, Liquid Death's commitment to sustainability and audacity underscores every aspect of its brand.

Next, brands must understand their audience deeply. Basecamp, the project management software company, prioritizes simplicity and usability over feature bloat, resonating with customers who value efficiency. Liquid Death taps into a younger demographic that seeks alternatives to sugary drinks and aligns with its humor and environmental focus.

Finally, brands must communicate consistently and be courageous. Occupy Wall Street, though not a brand in the traditional sense, owned its position unequivocally with its slogan, "We are the 99%." The movement's clear stance resonated globally, sparking conversations about economic inequality. Liquid Death's bold campaigns serve a similar purpose, reinforcing its message and rallying a community around shared values.

Owning your position is an ongoing process that requires vigilance, adaptability, and a willingness to stand firm in a world that pressures conformity. Liquid Death's success isn't just a story of edgy branding— it's a testament to the power of knowing who you are, what you stand for, and how to connect with the people who share your vision. In a marketplace crowded with options, it's the brands that dare to define themselves on their own terms that make the most lasting impact.

# Chapter 8
# Breaking the Unattainable Triangle

In the spring of 1974, a young engineer named Taiichi Ohno stood on the factory floor of Toyota's manufacturing plant in Japan. Post-war constraints had forced his team to rethink everything they knew about production. Resources were scarce, but the demand for quality vehicles was growing. Conventional wisdom said you couldn't have it all—you had to choose between quality, cost, or speed. But Ohno wasn't convinced. He found inspiration in an unexpected place: the just-in-time stocking methods of American supermarkets, where shelves were replenished only as products were sold, minimizing waste and excess inventory. What if car manufacturing could work the same way?

This question led to the creation of the Toyota Production System, a revolutionary approach that shattered the "Unattainable Triangle." Toyota found a way to produce high-quality cars both quickly and affordably, challenging the belief that you had to sacrifice one for the others. They didn't just improve an existing model—they reinvented it. Quality, cost, and speed were no longer mutually exclusive, and the rest of the automotive industry would never be the same.

Fast forward to the digital age, and we see similar stories of breaking constraints. In 2002, the aerospace industry was dominated by a few giants, and launching rockets was considered inherently expensive, slow, and complex. Elon Musk had a different vision for SpaceX. He wanted to reduce the cost of space travel by a factor of ten and do it faster than anyone thought possible. Critics were skeptical, citing the seemingly unbreakable trade-offs of the Unattainable Triangle. But Musk refused to accept these trade-offs. By designing reusable rockets and vertically integrating production, SpaceX slashed costs while speeding up development, all without compromising on quality. In 2015, they made history by landing the Falcon 9's first stage back on Earth—a feat that had previously been deemed impossible.

Dr. Govindappa Venkataswamy, or Dr. V, faced a different but equally daunting challenge in healthcare. Millions of people in India were needlessly blind due to cataracts, but most couldn't afford surgery. Conventional healthcare models could not solve this problem. So Dr. V created his own model with Aravind Eye Care, performing high-quality cataract surgeries at a fraction of the usual cost and at remarkable speed. Inspired by the efficiency of fast-food chains like McDonald's, he standardized procedures, trained specialized staff, and embraced a high-volume approach. The result was that Aravind Eye Care became the largest eye care provider in the world, restoring sight to millions without compromising quality or affordability.

These examples show that the Unattainable Triangle isn't a fixed law; it's a challenge waiting to be overcome. But for every success story, there are cautionary tales of brands that failed to strike the right balance. BlackBerry, for example, dominated the mobile communication market in the early 2000s by focusing on quality and security, but they ignored the need for speed in innovation. As competitors introduced faster, more adaptable devices, BlackBerry was unable to keep pace, and soon lost its grip on the market. The emphasis on quality alone wasn't enough to sustain them in a rapidly evolving landscape.

WeWork provides another example, this time of prioritizing speed at the expense of everything else. Leasing high-end office spaces and creating lavish work environments, it was about expanding quickly, without due attention to cost or the underlying quality of their business model. When plans for an IPO unraveled in 2019 that pursuit of growth without a solid foundation became evident. The emphasis on speed without regard to sustainability was a critical mistake.

The Occupy Wall Street movement also demonstrates the potential pitfalls of focusing solely on one aspect of the triangle—in this case, speed. In 2011, the movement mobilized quickly, capturing attention worldwide and sparking essential conversations about economic inequality. But the absence of structured goals and a lack of direction made it difficult for the movement to sustain itself. Despite resonating with millions initially, the inability to develop a strategy for long-term action meant that the momentum eventually dissipated, leaving its impact limited.

Warby Parker's journey offers a different perspective on breaking the constraints of the triangle in the retail space. Founded in 2010, Warby Parker sought to address the eyewear market's inefficiencies by delivering high-quality, stylish glasses at a lower price. Traditionally, eyeglasses were either expensive and stylish or cheap and unattractive. By cutting out middlemen and adopting a direct-to-consumer model, Warby Parker reduced costs while maintaining high quality. Their innovative Home Try-On program blended speed and convenience, allowing customers to test out frames at home. By refusing to accept the industry norms, they created an experience that felt personalized and accessible, effectively breaking the conventional trade-offs of the eyewear market.

Another example of breaking the triangle's constraints is Etsy. In 2005, Etsy created a global marketplace for handmade and vintage goods. Independent artisans often struggled with production speed and reaching customers while maintaining the uniqueness of their work. Etsy's platform allowed sellers to maintain quality and individuality while accessing a vast audience quickly and affordably. They redefined the Unattainable Triangle for independent creators, creating opportunities where the trade-offs seemed insurmountable.

The key takeaway is that challenging the traditional trade-offs requires a willingness to ask different questions and to seek inspiration in unexpected places. Brands like Toyota, SpaceX, Aravind Eye Care, Warby Parker, and Etsy did not simply choose two sides of the triangle—they reinvented the entire concept, proving that with creativity, it is possible to achieve quality, speed, and cost-efficiency simultaneously.

To achieve this, brands must start by understanding why they are scaling and what they aim to achieve. Tools like the Kano Model can help them hone in on what matters most to their customers, differentiating between basic expectations and features that excite. When considering speed, adopting an Agile approach allows teams to iterate quickly and adjust to changing demands. Lean Thinking, meanwhile, provides the foundation for reducing waste and maximizing value, ensuring that costs are kept in check without sacrificing quality.

The emergence of artificial intelligence has added a new dimension to breaking the Unattainable Triangle. AI has the power to be simultaneously faster, cheaper, and of higher quality, making it a unique tool in overcoming these trade-offs. AI-driven creative tools like Adobe Sensei analyze design trends and generate high-quality visual content, raising the bar for creative industries. In logistics, AI-powered systems can optimize delivery routes in real-time, enabling brands like Amazon to promise rapid delivery while keeping costs low.

AI has also enhanced healthcare, as demonstrated by DeepMind's AlphaFold, which has significantly accelerated the process of protein folding—an essential step in drug discovery. In education, AI-driven tools like Socratic by Google provide instant explanations to students, making high-quality tutoring accessible to more people. Vue.ai, an AI tool for fashion, provides personalized shopping experiences by analyzing user preferences, demonstrating how AI can improve the quality of customer interaction while also speeding up decision-making.

To break the Unattainable Triangle, brands need to combine intentionality, creativity, and the right tools. Leaders must begin by defining their ambitious north star and then use frameworks like Kano, Lean Thinking, and Agile to sharpen their focus. AI provides an unprecedented opportunity to revisit traditional constraints, empowering brands to redefine what is possible.

As we've seen through these stories, the Unattainable Triangle is not a limitation—it's an invitation to innovate. Whether it's leveraging just-in-time production to transform automotive manufacturing, reinventing healthcare with fast-food efficiency, designing affordable luxury eyewear, or using technology to expand access to niche goods, breaking through perceived constraints demands more than accepting trade-offs—it requires a shift in mindset. It requires the willingness to question assumptions, to look beyond conventional solutions, and to turn constraints into opportunities. By daring to break free from the limitations of the past, brands do more than succeed—they change the game entirely.

# Chapter 9
# Lazy Listening

In the early 2000s, a group of engineers at Google faced a perplexing challenge. They wanted to improve the relevance of search results, but traditional user surveys and focus groups weren't getting the insights they needed. Users struggled to articulate precisely what they wanted from a search engine—they simply knew when they found what they were looking for. So the team adopted a different approach. Instead of relying solely on users' verbal feedback, they turned their attention to behavior. They observed which search results were clicked, how often users returned to refine their queries, and patterns in how people phrased their searches. By "listening less" to what users said and paying more attention to what they did, Google refined its algorithms in transformative ways, changing how we access information forever.

This concept—gaining insights by stepping back and observing rather than actively probing—captures the essence of what I call "lazy listening." It is not about being indifferent or disengaged; it is about tuning into the subtle signals people send through their actions, signals that often reveal deeper truths than words can.

In the 1990s, LEGO faced a crisis. Sales were declining, and competition from video games was growing. Traditional market research seemed to point to a solution: children wanted more complexity and technological integration in their toys. LEGO responded by investing in advanced product lines packed with technological features, only to see those efforts fall short of expectations. It wasn't until LEGO's leadership decided to observe how children actually played that they uncovered the real insight. In homes around the world, they watched children engage most profoundly with simple bricks, creating entire worlds and embracing the freedom of open-ended play. This revelation led LEGO back to its roots, focusing on its core product—the classic brick. By encouraging creativity without overcomplicating the experience, LEGO reignited its appeal across generations.

Stepping back often reveals the most powerful insights.

In the bustling streets of Mumbai, the dabbawalas—lunchbox delivery men—operate a remarkably efficient system that delivers thousands of meals daily, with virtually no errors. Management experts from around the world have studied their methods, trying to understand the secret of their success. The dabbawalas, however, didn't optimize their system through elaborate meetings or detailed data analysis. Instead, they relied on a simple coding system of colors and symbols, honed over years of practical experience. Observing their workflow reveals a profound understanding of their environment and customers—an understanding that could never be captured through surveys or focus groups.

Sometimes, valuable insights come not from asking more questions but from paying closer attention.

Steve Jobs embodied this philosophy. He famously avoided traditional market research, convinced that customers often didn't know what they wanted until they saw it. When developing the iPhone, Apple did not conduct exhaustive surveys to determine whether people desired a touchscreen device without a physical keyboard. Instead, they observed the frustrations users had with existing smartphones and envisioned an elegant solution to address those pain points. This process resulted in a product that redefined the entire industry, a product born from attentively observing needs rather than explicitly asking about them.

Lazy listening isn't about ignoring the audience; it's about recognizing that actions speak louder than words. It's about creating the space for unspoken needs to reveal themselves. Charity: Water embraced this approach in their work to provide clean water to communities in developing countries. Instead of imposing preconceived solutions, they spent time within communities, observing how people collected water, understanding cultural nuances, and identifying the barriers to accessing clean water. By patiently listening through observation, Charity: Water implemented projects embraced and sustained by those communities, building solutions that lasted.

In business, there's often a compulsion to fill silence with noise, to gather data endlessly by asking question after question. But what if we took a step back? What if we allowed patterns to emerge naturally?

Fashion retailer Zara understands this well. Instead of relying solely on predictions of trends or designer intuition, they pay attention to what is selling in their stores on a weekly basis. They observe which items customers pick up, try on, and purchase. This real-time feedback directly informs their rapid design and production cycles, enabling them to deliver styles that resonate with consumers almost as fast as preferences shift. This approach has the added benefit of minimizing overproduction and reducing waste—an intelligent business move that aligns with environmental consciousness.

Cultivating lazy listening involves a few essential practices. First, it requires creating unobtrusive channels to observe customer behavior. Online platforms are treasure troves of data, capturing how users interact with products and services in real time. Analyzing this data reveals preferences, behaviors, and pain points that wouldn't necessarily surface in direct conversations. Second, embracing humility is critical. Recognizing that we may not always know the right questions to ask opens us up to unexpected insights that go beyond our preconceived notions. Finally, fostering a culture of observation is key—encouraging team members to immerse themselves in environments where the product is used, not to intervene but to quietly observe and learn.

Lazy listening is about finding wisdom in patience. It's about recognizing that sometimes, the most profound understanding comes not from pushing for answers but from letting them unfold naturally. In Japanese culture, there is a concept called "ma," which refers to the space between things—the silence between notes that gives music its depth. In communication, "ma" is the pause that lends words their meaning. By embracing this space, by allowing silence to speak, we create opportunities for deeper connections and insights.

In our drive to innovate and lead, embracing a bit more listening and a bit less talking might just be what we need. Sometimes, the answers we seek are already there, waiting for us to notice.

# Chapter 10

# **Adapt**

Deep in the heart of the Amazon rainforest lives a creature with an extraordinary gift: the glasswing butterfly. Its wings, almost entirely transparent, allow it to blend seamlessly with its environment. This isn't just a whimsical trait; it's a finely tuned survival mechanism perfected over millennia. By becoming nearly invisible, the glasswing avoids predators and thrives in a landscape teeming with threats. Nature, in its complexity, offers profound lessons on adaptation and resilience. It's not always the strongest species that survive; it's the ones that respond most effectively to change.

This principle resonates just as deeply in the world of brands and businesses navigating unpredictable landscapes. To thrive, brands must adopt a similar approach, blending flexibility and resilience into their core. Adaptation isn't just about survival—it's about leading the way into new frontiers.

On the streets of San Francisco, the future of transportation is quietly unfolding. Waymo's self-driving vehicles, including sleek all-electric Jaguar I-PACE cars, glide past, ferrying passengers without a human driver in sight. For those of us living in San Francisco, these cars have shifted from novelty to norm, a testament to how quickly new technologies can integrate into daily life.

For first-time riders, the experience is almost surreal—anticipation mingles with disbelief as the car navigates the city's complexities with precision. But as the ride progresses, that initial astonishment fades into an appreciation of what has been achieved: a smooth, reliable journey powered by cutting-edge technology. It's a glimpse of human ingenuity at its finest, and a reminder of how adaptation can create entirely new paradigms.

Jaguar's partnership with Waymo illustrates the transformation of a legacy brand into a forward-looking innovator. Once synonymous with luxury performance cars, Jaguar has embraced the electric and autonomous future with bold rebranding efforts. In 2024, the company unveiled its new logo and philosophy, "Exuberant Modernism," signaling a commitment to an all-electric lineup by 2025. Critics debated the aesthetics, but the message was clear: Jaguar is adapting not just to survive, but to thrive in a world reshaping the fundamental act of driving.

This rebrand represents more than a cosmetic update— it's a rallying cry for change. Love it or loathe it, Jaguar's evolution highlights the necessity for brands to address foundational shifts in their industries. As self-driving and electric technologies redefine transportation, Jaguar's pivot is a reminder that even the most storied brands must adapt to remain relevant.

Jaguar's transformation echoes the story of Interface, the global flooring company that turned to nature for guidance during its own reinvention. In the mid-1990s, Interface faced a crisis of conscience over its environmental impact. Founder Ray Anderson, inspired by the efficiency and diversity of natural ecosystems, introduced "Entropy," a line of carpet tiles mimicking the randomness of forest floors. This innovation not only reduced waste but also revolutionized the industry by aligning sustainability with product excellence.

Both Jaguar and Interface demonstrate that adaptation often requires looking outward—to the natural world, to shifting societal values, or to technological advancements—and inward, to core values that provide a foundation for change.

Adaptation isn't limited to technological innovation. In Nairobi's Kibera neighborhood, traditional infrastructure models often fail, but local ingenuity thrives. Sanergy, a community-driven organization, collaborates with residents to develop modular sanitation facilities tailored to the neighborhood's unique challenges. These solutions are cost-effective, scalable, and adaptable to changing conditions. By engaging directly with the community, Sanergy reflects the essence of true adaptation: meeting people where they are and evolving in response to their needs.

This bottom-up approach parallels how Mozilla operates. The open-source software company invites users and developers worldwide to contribute, creating a dynamic, decentralized model. Mozilla's adaptability stems from its ability to harness diverse perspectives and respond swiftly to technological changes and user needs.

For some brands, adaptation means stepping into entirely new domains. During the COVID-19 pandemic, Dyson, known for vacuums and air purifiers, pivoted to designing ventilators, leveraging its expertise in airflow technology to meet an urgent need. Similarly, Burberry repurposed its production lines to manufacture medical gowns and masks, applying its craftsmanship to serve a global crisis. Both brands demonstrated that adaptability doesn't require abandoning core competencies—it's about applying them in new, relevant ways.

Adaptation often starts with the right organizational structure. Spotify's "squad" model—small, autonomous teams responsible for specific product features—enables rapid iteration and continuous improvement. This decentralized approach mirrors natural systems like ant colonies, where adaptability arises from collective intelligence rather than rigid hierarchies.

The Morning Star Company, a tomato processor in California, takes this concept even further with its self-management model. By empowering employees to align their personal missions with company goals, Morning Star fosters a nimble, responsive organization capable of adapting without bureaucratic delays.

Adapting isn't just about responding to immediate challenges; it's about future-proofing through experimentation and resilience. Nassim Nicholas Taleb's concept of antifragility—systems that grow stronger under stress—offers a powerful framework for thinking about adaptation. Just as muscles grow through resistance and forests rejuvenate after fires, brands can use challenges as opportunities for growth.

AI provides a new frontier for adaptation. From predictive analytics to generative design, AI enables brands to iterate faster, explore speculative futures, and stress-test ideas. Imagine a world where AI identifies untapped intersections between industries, much like the partnership between Jaguar and Waymo. By leveraging AI as a tool for adaptation, brands can navigate uncertainty with greater agility.

Patagonia's Worn Wear initiative embodies adaptation at its finest. By encouraging customers to repair rather than replace their clothing, Patagonia aligned its operations with its environmental ethos, deepening customer loyalty. This approach exemplifies the principle that adaptation isn't about losing identity; it's about evolving into the most authentic version of what a brand was always meant to be.

Adaptation is a journey, not a destination. Whether it's Jaguar redefining luxury in the era of electric vehicles, Sanergy addressing infrastructure challenges, or Dyson pivoting to meet global needs, the ability to adapt is what separates enduring brands from those that fade into history. By looking to nature, embracing disruption, and fostering organizational resilience, brands can navigate change with confidence. In a world where the only constant is change, adaptation isn't just an advantage—it's a necessity.

# Chapter 11

# The Intersectional Advantage

In 1876, Alexander Graham Bell filed his patent for the telephone, narrowly beating Elisha Gray. Bell's vision for his invention transcended its technical specifications, driven by his background in speech therapy and electrical engineering. This intersectional lens enabled him to see the telephone not as a mere telegraph improvement but as a revolutionary communication tool. Gray, meanwhile, remained confined by the norms of his field, and history relegated him to a footnote. Bell's success illustrates the transformative power of intersections—moments when disciplines, ideas, and perspectives collide to create something groundbreaking.

Throughout history, these intersections have sparked innovation and progress, but failing to recognize their potential has cost some dearly. Polaroid, once a pioneer in instant photography, clung to its analog expertise even as digital technology reshaped the market. Entrenched in its comfort zone, the company missed the chance to marry analog gratification with digital tools, ultimately leading to its decline. Similarly, in the early days of climate research, siloed efforts between scientists and policymakers delayed meaningful action, as critical findings failed to reach decision-makers with the urgency they deserved.

In contrast, successes like Tim Berners-Lee's invention of the World Wide Web showcase the power of bridging disciplines. A physicist and computer scientist at CERN, Berners-Lee envisioned a universal system for sharing information across global research communities. His ability to integrate these domains laid the foundation for the modern internet, redefining communication and connectivity.

The principle of intersectionality is also evident in ecology through the "edge effect," where greater biodiversity flourishes at the boundaries of ecosystems, such as where a forest meets a grassland. This phenomenon reveals how blending different environments creates a space richer and more complex than the sum of its parts. Similarly, creativity thrives at the edges where disciplines, cultures, and ideas overlap.

One of the most contemporary and vivid examples of this intersectional dynamic is found in esports. The rise of platforms like Twitch has transformed gaming from a solitary hobby into a global spectacle. On Twitch, millions of viewers watch others play games they could play themselves. This shift reflects a deeper cultural phenomenon: gaming as performance, community, and storytelling.

The story of Twitch intersects with changes in how people experience entertainment. Watching others play offers more than the gameplay itself; it provides camaraderie, insights, and a shared narrative. For some, it's akin to attending a sports match or an interactive talk show. These virtual arenas have also become fertile ground for brands, with many finding innovative ways to connect with these communities.

Esports organizations and brands like Red Bull have embraced this evolution, sponsoring tournaments, streamers, and gaming content. Yet, there remains untapped potential for brands to engage more authentically. The unique intersection of gaming, storytelling, and community invites deeper exploration. Brands could lean into storytelling partnerships with gamers or integrate more participatory elements, allowing viewers to influence gameplay or narratives. Much like Bell's telephone or Berners-Lee's World Wide Web, this space is ripe for transformative ideas that bridge existing silos.

The lessons of intersectionality also resonate in business

practices. Airbnb's founders combined industrial design, technology, and hospitality to create a platform that redefined travel. Their insight into the intersection of practicality and human connection allowed them to tap into a desire for authentic experiences over standardized accommodations. Similarly, in culinary innovation, Chef Roy Choi's Kogi food trucks blended Mexican and Korean traditions, creating a fusion cuisine that reflected Los Angeles' diverse cultural fabric.

Brands and organizations seeking to harness these advantages can learn from IDEO's multidisciplinary approach. In 1999, IDEO assembled a team of diverse experts—from psychologists to engineers—to redesign the shopping cart. This convergence of perspectives led to a design that addressed safety, convenience, and usability in ways no single discipline could have achieved.

Tools like Google's "20% time" policy institutionalize the edge effect by encouraging employees to explore interests outside their core responsibilities. These initiatives foster cross-pollination, leading to innovations like Gmail and Google News. The AI-powered tool AlphaFold exemplifies this in healthcare, combining biology and machine learning to accelerate drug discovery by predicting protein structures—a feat previously thought insurmountable.

The rise of AI itself exemplifies the power of intersections. AI acts as an accelerant for blending fields, enabling rapid "what-if" scenario modeling or combining insights across disciplines in ways previously unimaginable. Tools like ChatGPT can map audience sentiment, stress-test speculative ideas, and propose innovative intersections for brands exploring new narratives or products.

The concept of intersectionality is also deeply personal. John Maeda's reflections on hybridity illuminate the creative power of living at the intersections of multiple identities and disciplines. Hybrids—those who don't belong to a single tribe—become bridge-builders, capable of connecting disparate ideas and generating novel solutions. Maeda emphasizes that such creativity requires intentional time for reflection and the courage to embrace complexity.

Brands looking to thrive at the intersection must start with clarity about their core values. Frameworks like Ikigai—representing the convergence of passion, mission, vocation, and profession—can guide teams to align their work with a higher purpose. The T-shaped skills model, championed by IDEO, offers another practical tool, encouraging deep expertise in one area while fostering curiosity and competency across others.

Bjork's genre-defying music embodies this philosophy. By blending electronic, classical, and indigenous influences, she creates art that is simultaneously innovative and authentic. Her work exists in a space between categories, demonstrating the transformative potential of the edge effect.

As boundaries between disciplines, industries, and cultures blur, the ability to navigate and create at these intersections becomes increasingly vital. Whether it's brands like TOMS combining commerce with philanthropy, or esports communities redefining entertainment, the edge of relevance is where the most profound opportunities lie.

The future belongs to those willing to step beyond their silos, embrace the unknown, and invite diverse perspectives into the fold. Because, as history and nature alike have shown, the richest possibilities emerge not in isolation, but at the intersections where worlds collide.

# Chapter 12:

# The Paradox of Expertise

In the late 19th century, Ignaz Semmelweis, a Hungarian physician, walked the halls of Vienna General Hospital, troubled by a deadly mystery. Women giving birth in the doctor's ward were dying at alarming rates from childbed fever, while those in the midwives' ward fared significantly better. Semmelweis observed that doctors often moved straight from autopsies to the delivery room without washing their hands. He hypothesized that invisible "cadaverous particles" were infecting the mothers.

To test his theory, he instituted a strict handwashing protocol using a chlorinated lime solution. The mortality rate plummeted. One might expect Semmelweis to be hailed as a hero, but instead, his findings were met with hostility. The medical community, confident in their expertise, dismissed his ideas. They couldn't fathom that they might be the source of the problem. Semmelweis's discovery challenged the established beliefs of the time, and rather than adapt, the experts entrenched themselves further.

This tragic story illustrates a paradox: expertise, while valuable, can sometimes blind us to new insights. The very knowledge and experience that make someone an expert can create barriers to change. Brands and organizations often face similar challenges, where success breeds complacency, and established ways of thinking hinder innovation.

Nokia dominated the mobile phone industry in the early 2000s. Nokia's engineers had perfected mobile phone technology and were the undisputed leaders in the field. But when smartphones began emerging—devices that were less about making calls and more about providing a platform for apps, media, and internet browsing—Nokia failed to adjust. Their expertise in hardware and traditional phone technology constrained their ability to envision the future of mobile as a software-driven, ecosystem-based experience. By the time they attempted to pivot, it was too late. Companies like Apple and Google had already reshaped the industry, and Nokia went from market leader to a cautionary tale in just a few short years.

Expertise can also create blind spots in science and technology. In the late 19th century, physicist Lord Kelvin confidently declared that "heavier-than-air flying machines are impossible." Kelvin was a leading scientist of his day, with groundbreaking contributions to thermodynamics. Yet, his expertise in existing scientific principles limited his ability to entertain new ideas in aerodynamics. He lacked the flexibility of thought that enabled the Wright brothers—who approached the challenge from the fresh perspective of bicycle mechanics—to prove him wrong and achieve powered flight.

The Wright brothers' story is echoed in the world of design by Dieter Rams. In the 1960s and 70s, Rams, a legendary designer for Braun, developed products that became icons of modern minimalism. But by the time the digital revolution rolled around, Braun's devotion to physical buttons, dials, and simplicity left them lagging behind newer players who embraced touchscreens and the digital interfaces that users increasingly demanded. Apple, a company whose design ethos had been influenced by Rams, took his ideas of simplicity and function and translated them into the digital era, while Braun struggled to adapt.

The Paradox of Expertise suggests that deep knowledge can foster complacency and create tunnel vision. To break free from these limitations, organizations must cultivate what Zen practitioners call a "beginner's mind." Shunryu Suzuki, a Zen monk, famously said, "In the beginner's mind there are many possibilities, but in the expert's mind there are few."

The beginner's mind is about approaching problems without preconceived notions, remaining curious and open to new ideas.

For brands and organizations, fostering a beginner's mindset means encouraging curiosity, questioning assumptions, and embracing diverse perspectives. A beginner's mindset can be cultivated through deliberate practice, starting with asking "dumb questions"—the questions that experts often dismiss. Dumb questions have the power to reveal blind spots, simplify complex concepts, and create space for novel approaches.

A powerful framework for cultivating a beginner's mindset is the "Five Whys" technique. Originally developed by Toyota for root cause analysis, the Five Whys encourage practitioners to keep digging deeper into a problem by repeatedly asking "why." This framework forces people to go beyond surface-level assumptions and can help dismantle the biases that come with expertise. For example, when faced with declining sales, asking "why" five times may reveal a much deeper issue than initially assumed—one that could range from customer dissatisfaction to a changing cultural landscape.

Another approach is the "Six Thinking Hats" method created by Edward de Bono. It encourages teams to look at problems from multiple perspectives by metaphorically wearing different hats: facts, emotions, caution, optimism, creativity, and management. This approach helps break out of the traditional confines of expertise and ensures that problems are seen through different lenses, promoting creative problem-solving and preventing groupthink.

It's also crucial for organizations to nurture an environment where dissenting opinions are valued. Pixar is a company that understands the pitfalls of expertise and has built a culture to counteract them. During the making of every film, Pixar employs a "brain trust" approach, where directors present their work to a group of peers who provide candid feedback. No matter how experienced or accomplished a director might be, the brain trust's purpose is to question, challenge, and provide a beginner's perspective that can lead to breakthroughs.

Another key to overcoming the limitations of expertise is to step outside the boundaries of one's industry. Elon Musk did this with Tesla. When the electric car company was founded, the automobile industry was largely driven by experts in mechanical engineering and traditional manufacturing. Musk, coming from a background in software and physics, approached car manufacturing differently. He saw the vehicle as not just a machine but as a sophisticated electronic system that could be upgraded, reprogrammed, and continually improved. Tesla's success wasn't just about creating a better electric car; it was about redefining what a car could be.

Similarly, in fashion, Virgil Abloh, an architect by training, brought his outsider perspective into the luxury fashion world. Abloh founded Off-White, a brand that defied the conventions of haute couture by blending streetwear influences with high fashion aesthetics. His approach disrupted the luxury industry and earned him a position as artistic director at Louis Vuitton. Abloh's success was a testament to the power of approaching a discipline from an unconventional angle— using expertise in one field to revolutionize another.

A modern example of breaking free from expertise comes from the gaming industry. When Nintendo faced the growing dominance of PlayStation and Xbox—both of which focused on increasing graphics power and technical capabilities— they took a different path. Instead of competing on the established expertise of high-performance consoles, Nintendo embraced simplicity and accessibility. The result was the Wii, a console designed for families and non-gamers. With motion controls and a focus on social play, the Wii redefined gaming for a broader audience, drawing in people who had never considered themselves gamers.

To embrace the beginner's mindset and question expertise, organizations can also leverage artificial intelligence. AI can serve as a tool to help question assumptions, generate fresh ideas, and provide alternative perspectives. For example, generative AI can be used in brainstorming sessions to propose product concepts or identify market opportunities that experts might overlook due to their ingrained biases. AI's ability to analyze vast datasets without preconceived notions allows it to identify patterns and connections that human experts might miss, particularly in domains where cross-disciplinary insights are needed.

AI can also support scenario planning by rapidly generating multiple future possibilities based on varying inputs, AI-generated simulations can help leaders visualize how different strategic choices could play out, offering insights that challenge the traditional expertise-based assumptions guiding decision-making. Whether in new product development, market expansion, or anticipating industry disruptions, AI can help organizations view the playing field with fresh eyes and make decisions that break free from the constraints of established expertise.

However, using AI effectively requires cultivating human oversight that embraces a beginner's mind. The insights generated by AI should be approached with curiosity rather than the automatic validation or dismissal that often accompanies expert analysis. This blend of human creativity, humility, and AI's expansive analytical power can help organizations navigate the paradox of expertise and unlock new opportunities.

The paradox of expertise teaches us that deep knowledge, while invaluable, can lead to overconfidence and narrow thinking. By encouraging a beginner's mindset, questioning assumptions, and inviting diverse perspectives, organizations can avoid the pitfalls of complacency. Expertise should be a foundation to build upon—not a fortress that keeps new ideas out.

Just as Ignaz Semmelweis's simple insight into hand hygiene could have saved countless lives if the medical community had been willing to listen, organizations today must be willing to look beyond their established knowledge. They must be open to learning from outsiders, from seemingly unrelated industries, and even from those with less experience.

In a rapidly changing world, those who balance expertise with humility, who remain open to questioning and curiosity, are the ones best positioned to not only adapt to change but to drive it.

Because sometimes, the greatest obstacle to innovation isn't ignorance—it's the illusion of knowledge.

# Chapter 13

# Embracing the Unconventional

In my career, I've often found myself doing two things: "weirding the normal" and "normalizing the weird." These two approaches aren't just clever phrases; they're strategies for transformative change. The act of taking something unusual and making it relatable, or reframing the mundane to be extraordinary, has driven some of the most significant innovations and brand successes in history. Being intentional about which of these challenges you're taking on—whether it's weirding the normal or normalizing the weird—means you can focus with precision, helping build a brand, product, or service that resonates deeply. Let me tell you a story.

Spring 1977 in a cluttered garage in Palo Alto, California. The Homebrew Computer Club—a group of hobbyists, engineers, and visionaries—gathered not just to build computers, but to redefine what they could be. This motley crew saw potential where others saw impracticality. Among them was a young Steve Wozniak, who would soon co-found Apple. At a time when computers were either colossal, inaccessible machines or speculative novelties, these tinkerers envisioned technology as deeply personal and within reach for everyone. They weren't motivated by commercial ambition but rather by a curiosity that led them to normal the weird—making personal computing seem possible and ultimately indispensable.

The same spirit of harnessing the unconventional has shaped movements across history. In the 1990s, the cypherpunk movement—a blend of cryptographers, privacy activists, and technology enthusiasts—advocated for strong encryption to protect civil liberties in the digital age. Their ideas were esoteric, misunderstood by many, and even viewed with suspicion by governments. But these cypherpunks didn't just innovate; they persevered, and their persistence laid the foundation for technologies like blockchain and cryptocurrencies. From the cryptographic theories of cypherpunks emerged Bitcoin—Satoshi Nakamoto's brainchild—a decentralized currency that challenged our traditional notions of value exchange and monetary control. It was a "weird" idea, one of fringe fascination, that gradually captured the public imagination and became a significant force in finance.

The process of translating fringe ideas into accessible narratives requires both skill and patience. Marcel Duchamp, an artist known for his unconventional approach, famously exemplified this. In 1917, he submitted "Fountain," a porcelain urinal signed "R. Mutt," to an art exhibition. The piece was rejected, yet it ultimately became one of the most significant works of modern art. Duchamp's use of "readymades" forced people to reexamine the very concept of art. His work was dismissed at first—deemed bizarre, even absurd—but over time, Duchamp redefined the rules, expanding the boundaries of artistic expression. He showed that the most impactful ideas often come from pushing against the established normal.

In the natural world, the Mexican axolotl provides a remarkable example of thriving through the unconventional. Unlike most amphibians, the axolotl remains in its larval stage throughout its life—a condition called neoteny. This perpetual youthfulness allows it to regenerate entire limbs, as well as parts of its brain and spinal cord, without scarring. Its weirdness is its strength, a trait that has captivated scientists, offering promising insights for human medicine. The axolotl refuses to follow traditional developmental patterns, and its refusal is what makes it an object of fascination and a symbol of the power that comes from embracing the unconventional.

Biomimicry takes inspiration from these oddities in nature to innovate. The design of Japan's Shinkansen Bullet Train drew inspiration from the kingfisher bird, whose beak shape allowed it to move efficiently between different air pressures without making noise. The boxfish—a seemingly impractical, boxy-looking creature—was the unlikely model for Mercedes-Benz engineers designing the Bionic concept car. The result was a vehicle that achieved an impressively low drag coefficient, translating the weirdness of nature into practical and efficient design. These examples show that the best lessons sometimes lie far outside the confines of traditional thinking.

In activist circles, unconventional approaches can often be catalysts for change. The Situationist International—a revolutionary group from the 1950s and 60s—challenged the monotony of modern life through playful, subversive actions. They coined the term "dérive" to describe an unplanned journey through urban environments, guided by aesthetic instinct rather than conventional purpose. This simple idea of experiencing a city differently was designed to undermine consumerist monotony and make people question the capitalist structures around them. The Situationists succeeded in planting seeds of discontent that echoed into movements like the 1968 Paris uprisings, reminding us that "weirding the normal" can be a powerful tool for sparking societal change.

In culture, the rise of Afrofuturism has blended elements of science fiction, fantasy, and African history to create new visions for the future of the African diaspora. Sun Ra, an early pioneer of Afrofuturism, claimed to be from Saturn and used his music to explore alternate realities. His work was a departure from conventional jazz, an unapologetically weird vision that reimagined the role of Black artists and philosophers. This form of expression, once niche, has become mainstream with films like "Black Panther," where speculative narratives address real-world issues of identity and inequality. Afrofuturism, through its fusion of the strange and the familiar, has demonstrated that unconventional perspectives can provide powerful platforms for social change.

Brands have much to gain from embracing the unconventional—not for novelty's sake, but as a strategic choice that differentiates and engages audiences. When Patagonia released an ad on Black Friday with the message "Don't Buy This Jacket," it wasn't just a statement. It was a provocative challenge to consumer culture and environmental irresponsibility. The weirdness of a company discouraging sales not only resonated with a specific set of values but reinforced Patagonia's positioning as a brand that puts the planet first. What seemed radical was, in fact, aligned perfectly with the emerging cultural shift toward sustainability. By weirding the normal, Patagonia turned what might have been an eccentric gesture into a symbol of authentic values that deepened customer loyalty.

Similarly, IKEA's introduction of flat-pack furniture was unconventional in its day. The idea that customers would willingly assemble their own furniture seemed outlandish, even intimidating. But IKEA did more than just introduce a product; they normalized the concept by creating clear, visual assembly instructions that made it accessible and even enjoyable. By embracing the weirdness of self-assembly, IKEA transformed a daunting idea into a cultural norm—one that emphasized affordability, practicality, and democratic access to well-designed furniture.

So how can brands effectively embrace the unconventional? First, they must be deliberate about which approach they are taking. Are they weirding the normal or normalizing the weird? This decision informs not only the direction but also the tools and strategies employed.

To help teams align on this choice, frameworks like "The Oblique Strategies" by Brian Eno can be useful. Originally created to help artists overcome creative blocks, these prompts offer unconventional ways to approach a problem—provoking thought in new directions that can help reveal whether to normalize the weird or make the normal seem extraordinary. Similarly, the "Jobs to Be Done" framework can help brands understand the core needs of their customers. By diving into what customers are really trying to achieve, teams can determine whether the unconventional aspect they're exploring truly resonates and offers meaningful value.

A simple method for figuring out the right strategy is to ask "What if?" questions. What if our brand decided to oppose consumerism? What if our product could regenerate like the axolotl? What if our service was approached not as an expert but as a newcomer? These "what ifs" can help reveal whether it's time to bring the fringe into the mainstream or reimagine something ordinary as radically different.

AI can play a powerful role in this process, helping teams stress-test their ideas. For example, generative AI can create prototypes or mock-ups that visualize what an unconventional approach might look like. Tools like GPT-4 can generate narrative scenarios that explore possible futures for a brand or simulate how different audiences might react to an unconventional product. AI can also assist in sentiment analysis, gauging reactions to unconventional ideas based on large datasets, which helps refine the narrative and design in ways that improve resonance.

The challenge lies in ensuring that these explorations maintain authenticity. Ethical considerations must guide the integration of unconventional elements. Brands must ask themselves: Does this unconventional move align with our core values? Is it done with intention, or is it merely for shock value? The aim is to ensure that any innovation— whether weirding the normal or normalizing the weird— resonates with the audience in a meaningful way.

Returning to the Homebrew Computer Club, it's clear that transformative change often begins with those willing to embrace the unconventional. What they envisioned in that Palo Alto garage wasn't just a new piece of hardware; it was a reimagining of the relationship between people and technology. Their gatherings planted the seeds of the personal computer revolution, which has since transformed every facet of modern life.

In a world that is oversaturated with information and choices, brands that dare to embrace the unconventional can truly stand out. By turning what others dismiss as eccentric or impractical into something indispensable, they invite people to see the world in new ways and participate in something larger than themselves. It's the power of reframing the strange as familiar, of taking a risk and inviting others to understand a new narrative.

Because often, the way to make the most impact isn't to follow the path already laid out—it's to walk the edge of what's possible, to bridge the gaps between the familiar and the unknown, and to boldly embrace what others overlook.

# Chapter 14

# Your Secret Weapon

In the depths of the Indonesian archipelago, there exists a creature that defies convention—the mimic octopus. Discovered only in 1998, this unassuming cephalopod possesses a remarkable ability: it can impersonate a host of other marine animals, from venomous lionfish to slithering sea snakes. By altering its shape, color, and behavior, the mimic octopus deceives predators and prey alike, leveraging its adaptability as a secret weapon for survival.

This extraordinary creature doesn't rely on brute strength or speed. Instead, it harnesses the power of transformation, turning disguise into an unfair advantage in the underwater world. The mimic octopus teaches us that in environments where resources are scarce and dangers abound, ingenuity can triumph over might.

In the realm of business and branding, similar principles apply. Organizations often seek that elusive edge—the unique insight, the proprietary process, the "secret sauce" that sets them apart from competitors. Framing innovation as a secret or unfair advantage isn't just a strategic maneuver; it's a way to galvanize teams around a shared mission, to inspire a collective belief in the exceptional value they bring to the world.

Signal operates with a clear mission: to provide secure communication accessible to everyone. Their commitment to open-source technology and end-to-end encryption is both their secret and their bet—a conviction that privacy is a fundamental right worth defending.

Signal's encryption protocols are widely regarded as some of the most secure in the industry. By making their code publicly available, they invite scrutiny and collaboration from experts worldwide. This transparency paradoxically strengthens their secret weapon, as continual refinement enhances their unfair advantage in a market dominated by tech giants with vast resources.

The team behind Signal is galvanized by more than just creating a successful product; they're driven by a cause. This alignment of purpose and innovation fosters a culture where every member understands the stakes and contributes to advancing their shared secret weapon.

In a different context, the Zapatista movement in the mountains of Chiapas, Mexico, illustrates how framing a unique approach as an unfair advantage can mobilize a community. Rising in 1994 in opposition to neoliberal policies and the marginalization of indigenous peoples, the Zapatistas combined traditional practices with modern technology, such as leveraging the internet to disseminate their message globally.

Their use of anonymity—embodied by the iconic masked figure of Subcomandante Marcos—served as both a protective measure and a unifying symbol. The masks weren't just disguises; they were a statement that the movement was about collective identity rather than individual leadership. This secrecy became their unfair advantage, confounding authorities and capturing the imagination of supporters worldwide.

The Zapatistas' innovative blend of indigenous wisdom and modern tactics allowed them to punch above their weight, influencing discourse on human rights and globalization far beyond their geographic confines.

In the corporate world, companies like SpaceX have reframed innovation as a bold bet—a daring gamble that, if successful, could redefine entire industries. When Elon

Musk announced the goal of colonizing Mars, it wasn't just a grand vision; it was a rallying cry. By setting seemingly impossible targets, SpaceX attracted top talent passionate about pushing the boundaries of what's possible.

Their development of reusable rockets, once considered unfeasible, became their unfair advantage. This breakthrough dramatically reduced the cost of space travel, positioning SpaceX ahead of traditional aerospace competitors. The company's secret wasn't hidden technology but a willingness to challenge entrenched assumptions and take risks others deemed too great.

This approach galvanized teams by instilling a sense of purpose and excitement. Employees weren't just working on rockets; they were contributing to humanity's future in space—a powerful motivator that transcended ordinary corporate objectives.

Nature offers further examples of unfair advantages born from unique adaptations. The pistol shrimp, a small crustacean, wields one of the most potent weapons in the animal kingdom. By snapping its claw at incredible speed, it creates a cavitation bubble that generates heat nearly as hot as the sun's surface and a shockwave that can stun or kill prey. This extraordinary ability allows the pistol shrimp to hunt effectively despite its diminutive size.

The pistol shrimp's secret isn't apparent at first glance, but it empowers the creature to thrive in competitive environments. Brands can draw inspiration from such adaptations by identifying and cultivating their own unique strengths—qualities that competitors can't easily replicate.

In the world of technology, Linux represents an unconventional secret weapon: the power of community collaboration. As an open-source operating system, Linux is developed by a global network of contributors who freely share code and improvements. This decentralized model allows for rapid innovation and adaptation, outpacing proprietary systems in certain domains.

Linux's unfair advantage lies in its collective intelligence and flexibility. Organizations that build on Linux, like Red Hat, have turned this community-driven innovation into successful business models, providing enterprise solutions while contributing back to the open-source ecosystem.

By framing their approach as a shared secret—a mutual investment in something greater than individual gain—these communities galvanize participants and create value that extends beyond traditional boundaries.

Activist movements often harness the concept of an unfair advantage through unconventional tactics. The Yes Men, a duo of culture jammers, employ impersonation and satire to expose corporate malfeasance and provoke public debate. By infiltrating conferences and media outlets posing as representatives of organizations like the World Trade Organization, they deliver outrageous statements that highlight real issues.

Their secret weapon is surprise—the ability to disrupt expectations and force audiences to confront uncomfortable truths. While their methods are controversial, the Yes Men effectively draw attention to topics that might otherwise be ignored, leveraging creativity as an unfair advantage.

So how can brands identify and leverage their own secret weapons?

Firstly, it requires introspection to uncover what truly sets an organization apart. This might be a proprietary technology, a unique cultural approach, or a visionary goal that others deem unattainable. The key is authenticity; the secret must be genuine and aligned with the brand's core values.

Secondly, framing this secret as an unfair advantage involves clear communication. It's about crafting a narrative that not only highlights the unique offering but also connects emotionally with stakeholders—employees, customers, investors—inviting them to be part of something special.

Thirdly, fostering a culture that embraces this secret

weapon is essential. Teams must understand and believe in the mission, seeing their roles as integral to advancing the collective advantage. This shared purpose can drive engagement, innovation, and resilience.

Finally, organizations should remain vigilant in nurturing and protecting their unfair advantage. Just as the mimic octopus continually adapts its disguises to navigate threats, brands must evolve their strategies to maintain their edge in changing environments.

Returning to the mimic octopus, we recognize that its success lies not in any single form it adopts but in its ability to transform as needed. Similarly, brands that cultivate a secret weapon rooted in adaptability position themselves to navigate uncertainty and seize opportunities that others might miss.

In a world where competition is fierce and attention spans are fleeting, leveraging a unique unfair advantage can make the difference between obscurity and prominence. Whether it's through groundbreaking technology, a unifying mission, or unconventional tactics, framing innovation in this way empowers organizations to galvanize teams and engage audiences on a deeper level.

Because sometimes, the most powerful strategy isn't about outmuscling the competition but outthinking them—finding that secret weapon that turns the tide in your favor.

# Chapter 15
# Go Rogue

In the late hours of a chilly November night in 1989, a young physicist named Tim Berners-Lee sat alone at his desk in Geneva's CERN laboratory. The room was cluttered with stacks of research papers, a humming computer terminal, and a restless energy borne out of frustration. The problem was simple yet profound: information silos were choking the potential for collaboration among scientists across the globe. Berners-Lee envisioned something radical—a system where documents could be linked seamlessly, accessible to anyone with a connection. This was the birth of the World Wide Web. It wasn't just a technological breakthrough; it was an act of rebellion against the established norms of how information was shared. Berners-Lee didn't wait for permission; he went rogue.

The idea was unconventional, and it disrupted everything. In that solitary moment of rogue creativity, he set in motion a transformation of how humanity communicates, learns, and evolves. Berners-Lee's audacity, his willingness to ignore convention and create something the world needed before it even knew it did, became a hallmark of what it means to "use design to design change." This spirit of audacious innovation—of challenging the status quo through design and intentional action—is the driving force behind resilient brands that thrive amid uncertainty. In times of ambiguity, it's the mavericks, the ones who color outside the lines, who redefine industries and reshape societies.

The Guerrilla Gardeners of South Los Angeles, led by Ron Finley. Frustrated by urban decay and the scarcity of fresh produce in their community, they took action. Under the cover of night, they transformed vacant lots and neglected medians into lush community gardens. These spaces, once symbols of neglect, became sources of nourishment and pride. This wasn't about asking for permission—it was about taking ownership. Their actions weren't just about planting vegetables; they were planting ideas, challenging systemic neglect and reimagining what urban spaces could be. By reclaiming public spaces, these rogue gardeners used design as a tool for social activism, fostering resilience in communities that had long been overlooked. It was a bold act of defiance wrapped in the quiet hope of growth.

The natural world offers its own lessons in the power of disruption and renewal. Certain fire-dependent ecosystems, like the lodgepole pine forests of North America, thrive on the periodic destruction of wildfires. For the lodgepole pine, fire is essential; its cones are sealed with a resin that only intense heat can open, releasing seeds to regenerate. What appears destructive on the surface is, in fact, life-giving. Fires clear out dense underbrush, recycle nutrients into the soil, and create the conditions for new growth. These ecosystems do not merely survive disruption—they embrace it, finding renewal and strength in unpredictability. They teach us that resilience is not about avoiding change but about thriving because of it.

Brands, too, can learn to not just weather disruptions but to embrace them as opportunities for reinvention. In the world of fashion, Vivienne Westwood stands as a powerful example of someone who used design to challenge norms and build resilience. Emerging from the punk scene of 1970s London, Westwood didn't just create clothes—she crafted narratives. Her garments were political statements, subversive and bold, questioning authority and championing individualism. Her brand's strength lies in its authenticity, its unwavering commitment to challenging the status quo. By consistently going against the grain, Westwood not only built an iconic fashion brand but also used design as a form of protest, keeping her work relevant through decades of change.

This ethos of going rogue is not about recklessness; it's about daring to question deeply held assumptions, to disrupt one's own models before external forces do it for you. Airbnb offers a perfect illustration of this concept. In 2007, Brian Chesky and Joe Gebbia needed to pay rent, so they decided to rent out air mattresses in their living room during a conference when hotel rooms were fully booked. What began as a scrappy solution to a personal problem soon grew into something much larger. By challenging the norms of the hospitality industry, Airbnb tapped into a latent desire for authentic experiences over sterile hotel accommodations. The founders went rogue by betting on the idea that people would welcome strangers into their homes—and they were right. Airbnb reshaped how we think about travel, community, and trust, using design to create connections where none previously existed.

Similarly, the origins of Burt's Bees lie in a kind of rogue thinking. Roxanne Quimby and Burt Shavitz started with candles made from leftover bee wax, operating out of an abandoned schoolhouse. Instead of chasing mass production, they embraced sustainability and natural ingredients—values that were unconventional at the time but resonated with an emerging market of environmentally conscious consumers. By staying true to their principles, Burt's Bees grew organically from a roadside honey stand to a global brand without sacrificing its authenticity. They thrived by embracing what others dismissed as fringe.

The hackerspace movement further embodies this ethos. Community-operated workshops like Noisebridge in San Francisco reject traditional hierarchies, providing spaces where individuals can experiment with computing, machining, and digital art. Born from hacker culture's emphasis on open sharing and hands-on creation, these spaces blur the lines between art and science, fostering radical inclusivity and collaborative innovation. Here, creativity isn't constrained by convention; it's amplified by the absence of it. Members work on projects ranging from robotics to biohacking, crafting change from the margins and proving that disruption can be deeply constructive.

The lessons are clear: whether in the streets of Los Angeles, the forests of North America, or the ateliers of London, resilience is built on the willingness to go rogue. It is about questioning assumptions, embracing disruption, and using design to create meaningful change. The greatest innovations often come from those willing to see the world differently and act on that vision. It is not about surviving uncertainty; it is about shaping it. By aligning our actions with purpose, fostering cultures of innovation, and leveraging design as a transformative tool, we can build organizations that don't just endure but define the future.

Go rogue. Use design to design change.

# Bibliography

# Launch

# The Power of "And"

### Airbnb's Origin
Discover how Brian Chesky and Joe Gebbia transformed a simple idea into a global phenomenon.

https://news.airbnb.com/about-us/

### Greta Thunberg's Climate Strike
Learn how a teenager's activism sparked a worldwide movement for climate justice.

https://www.ted.com/speakers/greta_thunberg

### Google Maps Launch
Explore how Google Maps revolutionized navigation and became an indispensable tool.

https://blog.google/products/maps/look-back-15-years-mapping-world/

### Zapatista Uprising
Understand the origins of the Zapatista movement and its fight for indigenous rights.

www.britannica.com/topic/Zapatista-National-Liberation-Army

### Tesla Roadster Launch
Discover how Tesla proved that sustainability and performance can coexist.

www.tesla.com/roadster

### Apple I Development
Apple combined technological innovation with user-friendly design to change the world, and share this moving, living memorial to Steve Jobs.

https://www.apple.com/stevejobs/

### Grameen Bank's Founding
Understand how microfinance helped millions escape poverty.

www.grameen.com/introduction

### Apollo Moon Landing
Reflect on how NASA achieved an unparalleled feat of exploration and engineering.

https://www.nasa.gov/mission/apollo-11/

### Warby Parker's Model
See how Warby Parker disrupted retail with a socially conscious business model.

https://www.warbyparker.com/history

# The Cultist Conundrum

**Apple's Cult Following**
Explore the psychology behind Apple's brand loyalty and cultural influence.

www.boldxcollective.com/insights-blog/cracking-the-code-of-apples-marketing-understanding-the-psychology

**CrossFit's Growth and Controversy**
Learn from CrossFit's meteoric rise and its subsequent challenges.

www.nytimes.com/2024/08/22/style/crossfit-games-death-crisis.html

**Patagonia's Environmental Activism**
Discover how Patagonia balances profit with purpose to create a mission-driven brand.

www.patagonia.com/activism

**Harley-Davidson's Community Building**
Understand how Harley-Davidson cultivated a passionate and enduring customer community.

www.harley-davidson.com/us/en/content/hog.html

**Theranos' Downfall**
Explore the consequences of unethical practices in a high-stakes corporate environment.

www.wsj.com/articles/theranos-has-struggled-with-blood-tests-1444881901

**REI's #OptOutside Campaign**
Learn how REI aligned their values with their brand, redefining retail practices.

www.rei.com/opt-outside

**Apple's Mission to "Think Different"**
See how Apple's ethos drives its innovation and market leadership.

https://www.apple.com/jobs/pdf/HBR_How_Apple_Is_Organized_For_Innovation-4.pdf

# Writing Your Legacy

**Jim Collins and David Packard's Philosophy**
Discover the principles of purpose-driven companies that endure for decades.

www.jimcollins.com/article_topics/ articles/good-to-great.html

**Yvon Chouinard's Transfer of Patagonia**
Learn how a company's ownership model can fight climate change.

www.patagonia.com/ownership

**Wangari Maathai and the Green Belt Movement**
Understand how grassroots efforts can restore ecosystems and empower women.

www.greenbeltmovement. org/wangari-maathai

**Muhammad Ali's Draft Refusal**
Reflect on the power of conviction in the face of immense opposition.

www.biography.com/ athlete/muhammad-ali

**Ben & Jerry's Social Activism**
Explore how a business integrates activism into its core values.

www.benjerry.com/values/ issues-we-care-about

**Steve Jobs' Vision for Apple**
Learn how design and simplicity redefined personal technology.

https://www.forbes.com/sites/ carminegallo/2011/01/18/steve- jobs-and-the-power-of-vision/

**Nelson Mandela's Legacy**
Gain insights into Mandela's journey from prisoner to president and global icon.

www.nelsonmandela.org/ content/page/biography

# Scale

**Facebook's Expansion**
Understand how Facebook transitioned from a college project to a global platform.

www.about.fb.com/company-info

**Five Guys Franchising**
Explore the strategies behind Five Guys' rapid expansion while maintaining quality.

www.fiveguys.com/the-five-guys-story

**Doctors Without Borders Principles**
Learn how core humanitarian values guide global healthcare efforts.

www.doctorswithoutborders.org/who-we-are

**WeWork's Rise and Fall**
Examine how ambition and mismanagement led to WeWork's dramatic decline.

www.nytimes.com/2019/09/25/business/wework-jpmorgan.html

**Netflix's Evolution**
Discover how Netflix reinvented entertainment through innovation and adaptability.

https://about.netflix.com/en

**Amazon's Infrastructure Investments**
Understand the role logistics and technology play in Amazon's scalability.

www.aboutamazon.com/about-us

**Airbnb's Community Building**
Explore how Airbnb invests in personal connections to maintain trust.

https://news.airbnb.com/brian-cheskys-open-letter-to-the-airbnb-community-about-building-a-21st-century-company/

# The Edge of Relevance

**Netflix's Evolution**
See how Netflix continually adapts to stay at the forefront of entertainment.

www.business.com/articles/ digital-disrupt-what-we-can-all- learn-from-the-netflix-model/

**Cirque du Soleil's Reimagined Circus**
Understand how creativity redefined a traditional art form.

www.cirquedusoleil.com/about-us

**Coca-Cola's AI Ad Controversy**
Explore the debates around Coca-Cola's AI-generated ad and its impact on creativity.

(search for analysis on TikTok and campaign critiques for further insight)

**Twitch Statistics**
Explore data behind Twitch's growth and its impact on the gaming industry.

www.statista.com/ statistics/1018251/twitch- streamers-hours-watched/

**Patagonia's Worn Wear Initiative**
Discover how Patagonia promotes sustainability through repair and reuse.

www.patagonia.com/worn-wear

**Supreme's Cultural Strategy**
Learn how Supreme created value through scarcity and cultural relevance.

www.gq.com/story/ inside-supreme

# Positioning

**Microsoft's Founding and Vision**
See the founding team
inspired by the January cover
of Popular Electronics

https://news.microsoft.com/
announcement/microsoft-is-born/

**Liquid Death's Story and Vision**
Understand how a bold brand
voice helped Liquid Death
disrupt the beverage industry.

www.liquiddeath.com/
pages/manifesto

www.marcom.com/liquid-
death-making-a-dumb-idea-
profitable-with-great-branding/

**Oatly's Brand Positioning**
Explore how Oatly turned oat
milk into a cultural phenomenon.

www.oatly.com/int/about-oatly

**REI's #OptOutside Campaign**
Learn how values-driven
branding positioned REI as
a leader in outdoor retail.

www.rei.com/opt-outside

**Nike's Colin Kaepernick Campaign**
Understand how Nike aligned
with cultural movements to
amplify its brand message.

www.nytimes.com/2018/09/04/
sports/nike-colin-kaepernick.html

**IKEA's Democratic Design**
Discover how IKEA's commitment
to affordability and functionality
drove global success.

www.ikea.com/us/en/
this-is-ikea/about-us/

**J.C. Penney's Failed Reinvention**
Learn the lessons of strategic
missteps in a retail transformation.

www.forbes.com/sites/
marketshare/2012/06/15/jc-
penneys-epic-rebranding-fail/

**Aesop's Brand Identity**
Explore the meticulous
philosophy and unique
storytelling behind Aesop.

www.aesop.com/us/r/about/

**Occupy Wall Street's Position**
Understand the messaging and
cultural impact of the Occupy
Wall Street movement.

www.britannica.com/event/
Occupy-Wall-Street

# Breaking the Triangle

## Toyota Production System
Discover how Toyota revolutionized manufacturing through efficiency and innovation.

www.toyota-global.com/
company/vision_philosophy/
toyota_production_system

## SpaceX's Reusable Rockets
Learn how SpaceX reduced costs and expanded access to space exploration.

www.spacex.com/
vehicles/falcon-9

## Aravind Eye Care
Understand how Aravind provides high-quality, affordable healthcare at scale.

www.aravind.org

## Warby Parker's Model
Explore how a commitment to style and social good transformed eyewear.

www.warbyparker.com/history

## Etsy's Marketplace
See how Etsy connects independent artisans with global audiences.

www.etsy.com/about

## Adobe Sensei
Discover how Adobe integrates AI to enhance creativity and content quality.

www.adobe.com/sensei

## DeepMind AlphaFold
Learn how AI predicts protein folding, revolutionizing healthcare.

www.deepmind.com/research/
case-studies/alphafold

## Vue.ai in Fashion
Explore how AI personalizes shopping experiences in the fashion industry.

www.vue.ai

# Lazy Listening

**Google's Search Algorithm Development**
Understand how user behavior improves search relevance.

www.google.com/search/howsearchworks

**LEGO's Return to Core Products**
Learn how LEGO refocused on its original strengths to recover and thrive.

www.lego.com/en-us/history

**Mumbai's Dabbawalas Efficiency**
Discover lessons in precision and reliability from Mumbai's legendary delivery system.

www.forbes.com/sites/peterhigh/2015/02/23/the-best-logistics-organization-in-india-uses-no-technology-and-a-mostly-illiterate-workforce/

**Steve Jobs on Market Research**
Explore Jobs' belief in intuition over traditional market research.

www.inc.com/jason-aten/this-was-steve-jobs-most-controversial-legacy-it-was-also-his-most-brilliant.html

**Charity: Water's Community Engagement**
Learn how understanding local needs leads to impactful solutions.

www.charitywater.org/our-work

**Zara's Real-Time Fashion Model**
Understand how Zara uses data to inform fast and responsive fashion.

https://store.hbr.org/product/zara-fast-fashion/703497?srsltid=AfmBOoo3cc_bJFR8bFo1EeAeT-_iIb8vq1-4AHssNbowP_DWHPVZLmkg

**Concept of "Ma" in Japanese Culture**
Explore the Japanese philosophy of space and pause in communication and design.

www.japanhousela.com/articles/a-perspective-on-the-japanese-concept-of-ma/

# Adapt

**Jaguar and Waymo Collaboration**
Learn how partnerships drive innovation in self-driving technology.

https://media.jaguar.com/news/2018/03/waymo-and-jaguar-land-rover-announce-long-term-partnership-beginning-self-driving

**Jaguar Rebrand**
Understand how Jaguar is embracing a bold, all-electric future.

www.jaguarusa.com/copy-nothing/jaguar-type-00.html

**Interface and Biomimicry**
Explore how sustainable design can draw inspiration from nature.

https://blog.interface.com/future-of-design-biomimicry/

**Sanergy in Kibera**
Learn how community-driven sanitation solutions can transform urban areas.

www.saner.gy

**Mozilla's Open-Source Philosophy**
Understand Mozilla's collaborative approach to adaptability.

www.mozilla.org/en-US/about

**Dyson's Ventilator Production**
Discover how Dyson pivoted to address urgent healthcare needs during the pandemic.

www.dyson.co.uk/discover/archive/2020/ventilator-update

**Spotify's Agile Structure**
Explore how Spotify's organizational model supports innovation.

www.atlassian.com/agile/agile-at-scale/spotify

**Patagonia's Worn Wear Initiative**
See how Patagonia encourages repair over replacement for sustainability.

www.patagonia.com/worn-wear

# The Intersectional Advantage

**Tim Berners-Lee and the World Wide Web**
Learn about the origins of the internet and its visionary creator.

www.webfoundation.org/about/vision/history-of-the-web

**IDEO's Shopping Cart Redesign**
Understand the power of multidisciplinary approaches in solving complex problems.

www.ideo.com/journal/reimagining-the-shopping-cart

**Edge Effect in Ecology**
Discover how biodiversity thrives at ecosystem boundaries.

www.britannica.com/science/edge-effect

**Kogi Korean BBQ Fusion Cuisine**
Explore how Chef Roy Choi revolutionized street food with cultural fusion.

www.kogibbq.com/about

**Twitch and Esports Communities**
Learn how gaming platforms create global communities and brand engagement.

https://tesi.luiss.it/40175/1/275071_NAVIGLI_ALESSIA.pdf

**Ikigai Framework**
Understand the Japanese concept of finding purpose in life and work.

www.bbc.com/worklife/article/20170807-ikigai-a-japanese-concept-to-improve-work-and-life

**TOMS Shoes' One-for-One Model**
Explore how TOMS combines commerce with philanthropy.

www.toms.com/us/about-toms.html

**DeepMind AlphaFold**
See how AI is reshaping scientific research and healthcare.

www.deepmind.com/research/case-studies/alphafold

**John Maeda on Hybridity**
Learn how intersecting disciplines fuel creativity and innovation.

https://johnmaeda.medium.com/embracing-the-hybrid-path-reflections-on-creativity-career-and-resilience-8e72a3e87d52

# The Paradox of Expertise

**Ignaz Semmelweis and Handwashing**
Discover how early insights into hygiene were resisted by the medical community.

www.britannica.com/biography/Ignaz-Semmelweis

**Nokia's Decline in the Mobile Market**
Understand how failure to adapt led to the downfall of a once-dominant brand.

https://www.bbc.com/news/technology-23947212

**Lord Kelvin's View on Flight**
Learn from history's skepticism toward innovation, such as Kelvin's disbelief in aviation.

www.history.com/news/10-things-you-may-not-know-about-the-wright-brothers

**Dieter Rams and Braun**
Explore the challenges of maintaining minimalist design principles in a digital era.

https://us.braun.com/en-us/design/design-and-innovation

**Five Whys Technique**
Understand Toyota's simple yet powerful method for identifying root causes.

www.mindtools.com/aph6b8q/5-whys-video

**Six Thinking Hats**
Learn Edward de Bono's decision-making tool to foster creativity and collaboration.

www.debonogroup.com/services/core-programs/six-thinking-hats

**Pixar's Brain Trust**
Explore Pixar's innovative feedback system that drives creative excellence.

www.forbes.com/sites/gregsatell/2015/05/29/the-little-known-secret-to-pixars-creative-success/

**Elon Musk and Tesla's Approach**
Discover how an outsider perspective transformed the car industry.

https://www.wired.com/2010/09/ff-tesla/

# Embracing the Unconventional

**Virgil Abloh and Off-White**
Learn how Abloh merged architecture and fashion to redefine luxury.

www.gq.com/story/virgil-abloh-design-legacy

**Nintendo Wii's Success**
See how Nintendo disrupted gaming with a focus on accessibility and simplicity.

https://hbr.org/2010/08/what-can-we-learn-from-ninten

**Homebrew Computer Club**
Explore how Silicon Valley's hobbyists shaped the personal computer revolution.

www.computerhistory.org/revolution/personal-computers/17/312

**Cypherpunk Movement**
Understand the roots of cryptography and privacy advocacy.

www.wired.com/1993/02/crypto-rebels

**Satoshi Nakamoto and Bitcoin**
Discover how blockchain technology transformed digital finance.

www.bitcoin.org/en/bitcoin-paper

**Marcel Duchamp's "Fountain"**
Learn how Duchamp's provocative art challenged conventions and redefined modern art.

www.tate.org.uk/art/artworks/duchamp-fountain-t07573

# The Paradox of Expertise

**Axolotl's Regeneration Abilities**
See how this unique species
inspires research into
regenerative medicine.

www.nationalgeographic.com/
animals/amphibians/a/axolotl

**Mercedes-Benz Bionic Car
Inspired by Boxfish**
Discover how biomimicry led to
innovations in automotive design.

group.mercedes-benz.com/
sustainability/resources-
circularity/materials/
bionic-components.html

**Situationist International
and the Dérive**
Understand how urban exploration
challenges conventional views
of space and society.

www.theartstory.org/movement/
situationist-international

**Sun Ra and Afrofuturism**
Explore how Sun Ra blended
music and philosophy to influence
the Afrofuturism movement.

https://www.npr.org/sections/
logsupreme/2014/05/22/314363815/
act-like-you-know-sun-ra

**Patagonia's "Don't Buy
This Jacket" Ad**
Learn how Patagonia used
advertising to promote
environmental responsibility.

www.patagonia.com/stories/
dont-buy-this-jacket-black-
friday-and-the-new-york-
times/story-18615.html

**IKEA's Flat-Pack
Furniture Innovation**
See how self-assembly
furniture revolutionized retail
and democratized design.

www.ikea.com/ph/en/this-is-
ikea/about-us/the-story-of-
ikea-flatpacks-puba710ccb0/

# Your Secret Weapon

**Mimic Octopus Discovery and Abilities**
Discover the mimic octopus's remarkable ability to impersonate predators and prey.

www.nationalgeographic.com/
animals/invertebrates/m/
mimic-octopus

**Signal Messaging App**
Understand how Signal prioritizes privacy and security in digital communication.

https://github.com/signalapp

**Zapatista Movement**
Explore how the Zapatistas advocated for indigenous rights and autonomy.

www.culturalsurvival.org/
news/hidden-faces-zapatista-
army-national-liberation

**SpaceX and Reusable Rockets**
See how SpaceX redefined space travel through cost-efficient technology.

www.spacex.com/
vehicles/falcon-9

**Pistol Shrimp's Cavitation Bubble**
Learn about the shrimp's extraordinary ability to create shockwaves with its claw.

www.scientificamerican.com/
article/snapping-shrimp/

**Linux Operating System and Open Source**
Understand how open-source collaboration led to the development of Linux.

www.linuxfoundation.org

**Red Hat's Business Model**
Explore how Red Hat transformed open source into a successful enterprise solution.

www.redhat.com/en/
about/company

**The Yes Men and Culture Jamming**
Learn how the Yes Men use humor and pranks to spotlight social and political issues.

www.theyesmen.org

# Go Rogue

**Tim Berners-Lee and the Creation of the World Wide Web**
Discover how Berners-Lee developed the technologies that revolutionized communication.

www.w3.org/People/Berners-Lee

**Guerrilla Gardening Movement and Ron Finley**
Explore how activists reclaim urban spaces through gardening.

www.ronfinley.com

**Hackerspaces and Noisebridge**
Learn how community-run spaces foster collaboration and innovation.

www.noisebridge.net/wiki/Noisebridge

**Fire-Dependent Ecosystems**
Understand how certain ecosystems rely on periodic fires for regeneration.

https://smokeybear.com/en/about-wildland-fire/benefits-of-fire/fire-in-nature

**Vivienne Westwood's Impact on Fashion**
See how Westwood redefined fashion by merging punk aesthetics with high fashion.

www.viviennewestwood.com/sustainability/

**Airbnb's Origin Story**
Discover how creativity and grit turned air mattresses into a billion-dollar idea.

news.airbnb.com/about-us/

**Burt's Bees Founding and Growth**
Learn how Burt's Bees turned natural ingredients into a beloved brand.

www.burtsbees.com/our-story

Use design
to design
change

www.ingramcontent.com/pod-product-compliance
Lightning Source LLC
Chambersburg PA
CBHW070434290526
45791CB00005B/1969